ESSENTIAL LIBERTY

"They who can g[...]
temporary safet[...]

This refere[...]
as "endowed [...]
Founders in the [...] of Independence and
the U.S. Constitution. It is a publication of the
Essential Liberty Project, supporting the restoration
of constitutional integrity and Rule of Law, and includes
a comprehensive introduction on The Legacy of
American Liberty by Mark Alexander,
Publisher of *The Patriot Post* (PatriotPost.US).

Essential Liberty may be purchased and/or sponsored for
distribution to students, grassroots organizations, civic
clubs, political alliances, military and public service
personnel, and other groups. This guide and other
resources are also available in free downloadable formats.

For more information, visit EssentialLibertyProject.US

Written, designed and produced in the USA.
© 2009 Publius Press, Inc. All Rights Reserved.

ISBN 10: 0-615-30172-X
ISBN 13: 978-0-615-30172-3

TABLE OF CONTENTS

THE LEGACY OF AMERICAN LIBERTY
BY MARK ALEXANDER

Sons of Liberty

On December 16th, 1773, "radicals" from Boston, Massachusetts, members of a secret organization of American Patriots called Sons of Liberty, boarded three East India Company ships and threw into Boston Harbor 342 chests of tea. This iconic event, in protest of oppressive British taxation and tyrannical rule, became known as the Boston Tea Party.

Resistance to the Crown had been mounting over enforcement of the 1764 Sugar Act, 1765 Stamp Act and 1767 Townshend Acts, which led to the Boston Massacre, and gave rise to the slogan "No taxation without representation." The 1773 Tea Act and resulting Tea Party protest galvanized the Colonial movement opposing British parliamentary acts, which violated the natural, charter, and constitutional rights of colonists.

In response to the rebellion, the British enacted additional punitive measures, labeled the "Intolerable Acts," in hopes of suppressing the insurrection. Far from accomplishing that outcome, the Crown's countermeasures led Colonists to convene the First Continental Congress on September 5th, 1774 in Philadelphia.

Representatives from 12 of the 13 colonies (Georgia did not send delegates) drafted a list of rights and grievances with a request for redress from King George, and they agreed to an economic boycott of England to compel the Crown to concede. Congress also agreed to convene a Second Continental Congress if their grievances were not resolved.

Though the boycott reduced British imports by more than 90 percent, Royalists countered with vigorous enforcement of the Intolerable Acts.

On April 19th, 1775, Paul Revere departed Charlestown (near Boston) for Lexington and Concord in order to warn John Hancock, Samuel Adams and other Sons of Liberty that the British army was marching to arrest them and seize their weapons caches. While Revere was captured after reaching Lexington, his friend, Samuel Prescott, took word to the militiamen at Concord.

In the early dawn of that first Patriots' Day, Captain John Parker, commander of the Lexington militia, ordered, "Don't fire unless fired upon, but if they want a war let it begin here." And it did – American Minutemen fired the "shot heard round the world," as immortalized by poet Ralph Waldo Emerson, confronting British Regulars on Lexington Green and at Concord's Old North Bridge.

Thus, by the time the Second Continental Congress was convened on May 10th, 1775, the young nation was in open war.

On May 15th, Congress adopted a resolution calling on the states to prepare for rebellion. In its preamble, John Adams advised his countrymen to sever all oaths of allegiance to the Crown.

Most notably, on July 6th, Congress approved the "Declaration of the Cause and Necessity of Taking up Arms," drafted by Thomas Jefferson and John Dickinson, which noted: "With hearts fortified with these animating reflections, we most solemnly, before God and the world, declare, that, exerting the utmost energy of those powers, which our beneficent Creator hath graciously bestowed upon us, the arms we have been compelled by our enemies to assume, we will, in defiance of every hazard, with unabating firmness and perseverance employ for the preservation of our liberties; being with one mind resolved to die freemen rather than to live as slaves."

Samuel Adams proclaimed, "[T]he people alone have an incontestable, unalienable, and indefeasible right to institute government and to reform, alter, or totally change the same when their protection, safety, prosperity, and happiness require it."

"Endowed by their Creator"

A year later in Philadelphia, on July 4th, 1776, Jefferson and 55 merchants, farmers, doctors, lawyers and other representatives of the original 13 colonies of the United States of America, in the General Congress, Assembled, pledged "our lives, our fortunes and our sacred honor" to the cause of liberty. They declared, "When in the Course of human events, it becomes necessary for one people to dissolve the political bands which have connected them with another, and to assume among the powers of the earth, the separate and equal station to which the Laws of Nature and of Nature's God entitle them, a decent respect to the opinions of mankind requires that they should declare the causes which impel them to the separation."

Our Founders further avowed, "We hold these truths to be self-evident, that all men are created equal, that they are endowed by their Creator with certain unalienable Rights, that among these are Life, Liberty and the pursuit of Happiness. That to secure these rights, Governments are instituted among Men, deriving their just powers from the consent of the governed, That whenever any Form of Government becomes destructive of these ends, it is the Right of the People to alter or to abolish it, and to institute new Government, laying its foundation on such principles and organizing its powers in such form, as to them shall seem most likely to effect their Safety and Happiness."

Our Declaration of Independence was derived from common law, "the Laws of Nature and Nature's God," all men being "endowed by their Creator with certain unalienable Rights." It calls upon "the Supreme Judge of the world for the rectitude of our intentions" and "the protection of Divine Providence."

The Declaration's common law inspiration for the Rights of Man has its origin in governing documents dating back to the *Magna Carta* (1215), and was heavily influenced by the writings of Charles Montesquieu and John Locke.

However, its most immediate common law inspiration was William Blackstone's 1765 "Commentaries on the Laws of England," perhaps the most scholarly historic and analytic treatise on Natural Law.

Blackstone wrote, "As man depends absolutely upon his Maker for everything, it is necessary that he should in all points conform to his Maker's will. This will of his Maker is called the law of nature. ... This law of nature, being coeval [coexistent] with mankind and dictated by God Himself is, of course, superior in obligation to any other. It is binding over all the globe, in all countries, and at all times; no human laws are of any validity if contrary to this. ... Upon these two foundations, the law of nature and the law of revelation, depend all human laws; that is to say, no human laws should be suffered [permitted] to contradict these."

In 1776, the Second Continental Congress appointed a committee representing the 13 states to draft a formal document of incorporation, and then approved the Articles of Confederation and Perpetual Union for ratification by the states on November 15th, 1777. The Articles of Confederation were ratified on March 1st, 1781, and "the United States in Congress assembled" became the Congress of the Confederation.

"We the People"

At the conclusion of the Revolutionary War, it was evident that the Articles of Confederation between the states did not sufficiently ensure the interests and security of the Confederation. In September 1786, at the urging of James Madison, 12 delegates from five states (New Jersey, New York, Pennsylvania, Delaware and Virginia) met in Annapolis, Maryland, to consider amendments to the Articles.

Those delegates called for representatives from all of the states to convene at the Pennsylvania State House in Philadelphia for full consideration of the revisions needed, and 12 states (Rhode Island declining) sent 55 delegates, a third of whom signed the Declaration of Independence.

The most noted delegates were George Washington, Roger Sherman, Alexander Hamilton, Benjamin Franklin, James Madison and George Mason. (Thomas Jefferson was in Europe in his capacity as Minister to France, but in correspondence with Madison, expressed his cautious support for the new Constitution.)

Noticeably absent from the proceedings were Patrick Henry, Samuel Adams and Thomas Paine, who believed the Articles did not need replacement, only modification. They were concerned that a proceeding aimed at establishing a new constitution could place in peril our fundamental liberties. Summing up their sentiments, Henry wrote that he "smelt a rat in Philadelphia, tending toward the monarchy."

The Philadelphia Convention (Constitution Convention) opened its proceedings on May 25th, 1787, and soon decided against amending the existing Articles in favor of drafting a new constitution. The next three months were devoted to deliberations on various proposals with the objective of drafting a document, which would secure the rights and principles enumerated in the Declaration and Articles of Confederation, thus preserving essential liberty.

In late July, after much debate, a Committee of Detail was appointed to draft a document to include all the compromise agreements, but based primarily on James Madison's Virginia Plan, establishing a republican form of government subject to strict Rule of Law, reflecting the consent of the people and severely limiting the power of the central government.

A month later, the Committee of Style and Arrangement, which included Gouverneur Morris, Alexander Hamilton, William Samuel Johnson, Rufus King and James Madison, produced the final draft of the Constitution, which was submitted for delegate signatures on September 17th, 1787.

George Washington and the delegates to the Convention wrote, "We the People of the United States, in Order to form a more perfect Union, establish Justice, insure domestic

Tranquility, provide for the common defence, promote the general Welfare, and secure the Blessings of Liberty to ourselves and our Posterity, do ordain and establish this Constitution for the United States of America."

Said Benjamin Franklin of the new document, "I confess that there are several parts of this constitution which I do not at present approve, but I am not sure I shall never approve them: For having lived long, I have experienced many instances of being obliged by better information, or fuller consideration, to change opinions even on important subjects, which I once thought right, but found to be otherwise. ... Thus I consent, Sir, to this Constitution because I expect no better, and because I am not sure, that it is not the best."

Of the 55 delegates, 39 signed the new Constitution while the remaining delegates declined, most out of concern that the power apportioned through the new plan was a threat to the sovereignty of the several states, and thus, to individual liberty.

The ensuing ratification debates among the states were vigorous.

James Madison, John Jay and Alexander Hamilton authored *The Federalist Papers* advocating ratification of the new Constitution.

Patrick Henry's Anti-Federalists opposed the plan under consideration because they believed it allocated too much power to the central government. Henry, Samuel Adams, George Mason, Robert Yates, Thomas Paine, Samuel Bryan and Richard Henry Lee were among those who spoke against ratification, and some authored several essays that were aggregated and published as *The Anti-Federalist Papers*.

The new Constitution stipulated that once nine of the 13 original States ratified it through state conventions, a date would be established for its implementation. This created controversy, as the document in question had no standing authority to make such a stipulation. However, once the ninth state, New Hampshire, reported its convention's approval on June 21st, 1788, the Continental Congress set the date for enactment of the Constitution for March 4th, 1789.

With Rhode Island's ratification on May 29th, 1790, all 13 states had endorsed the Constitution.

Though critical of many of its provisions, in reflection Thomas Jefferson wrote of the Convention and its product, "The example of changing a constitution by assembling the wise men of the state, instead of assembling armies, will be worth as much to the world as the former examples we had given them. The constitution, too, which was the result of our deliberation, is unquestionably the wisest ever yet presented to men."

"To secure these rights"

"In order to prevent misconstruction or abuse of [the Constitution's] powers..." –Preamble to the Bill of Rights

Endeavoring to further define our Constitution's limits on government encroachment upon the innate Rights of the People, James Madison, its primary architect, introduced to the First Congress in 1789, a Bill of Rights – the first 10 Amendments to our Constitution, which was then ratified on December 15th, 1791.

The Bill of Rights was inspired by three remarkable

documents: Two Treatises of Government, authored by John Locke in 1689 regarding protection of "property" (in the Latin context, proprius, or one's own "life, liberty and estate"); the Virginia Declaration of Rights, authored by George Mason in 1776 as part of that state's constitution; and, of course, our Declaration of Independence, authored by Thomas Jefferson.

There was great consternation regarding the enumeration of these rights, as such registration might be taken to suggest that they were subject to amendment rather than unalienable; granted by the state rather than "Endowed by [our] Creator."

As Hamilton argued in Federalist No. 84, "Bills of rights, in the sense and to the extent in which they are contended for, are not only unnecessary in the proposed Constitution, but would even be dangerous. ... For why declare that things shall not be done which there is no power to do?"

On the other hand, George Mason was among 16 of the 55 Constitution Convention delegates who refused to sign because the document did not adequately address limitations on what the central government had "no power to do." Indeed, he worked with Patrick Henry and Samuel Adams against its ratification for that reason.

As a result of Mason's insistence, the first session of Congress placed these 10 additional limitations upon the federal government for the reasons outlined by the Preamble to the Bill of Rights: "The Conventions of a number of the States having at the time of their adopting the Constitution, expressed a desire, in order to prevent misconstruction or abuse of its powers, that further declaratory and restrictive clauses should be added:

And as extending the ground of public confidence in the Government, will best insure the beneficent ends of its institution..."

Read in context, the Bill of Rights is both an affirmation of innate individual rights (as noted by Thomas Jefferson: "The God who gave us life gave us liberty at the same time") and a clear delineation of constraints upon the central government.

The Rule of Law

"But where say some is the King of America? I'll tell you Friend, he reigns above, and doth not make havoc of mankind... Let it be brought forth placed on the divine law, the word of God; let a crown be placed thereon, by which the world may know...that in America THE LAW IS KING."
–Thomas Paine

For its first 150 years (with a few exceptions), our Constitution stood as our Founders and "the people" intended – as is – in accordance with its original intent. In other words, it was interpreted exegetically rather than eisegetically – textually as constructed, rather than as a so-called "living" document, altered to express the biases of later generations of politicians and jurists.

But incrementally, constitutional Rule of Law in the United States has been diluted by unlawful actions of those in the executive, legislative and judicial branches – most notably, the latter – at great hazard to the future of liberty.

As Thomas Jefferson warned repeatedly, the greatest threat to the Rule of Law and constitutional limitations on central government was an unbridled judiciary: "The original error [was in] establishing a judiciary independent of the nation, and which, from the citadel of the law, can turn its guns on those they were meant to defend, and control and fashion their proceedings to its own will. ... The opinion which gives to the judges the right to decide what laws are constitutional and what not, not only for themselves in their own sphere of action but for the Legislature and Executive also in their spheres, would make the Judiciary a despotic branch."

Jefferson understood that should our Constitution ever become a straw man for a politicized judiciary to interpret as it pleased, Rule of Law would gradually yield to rule of men – the terminus of the latter being tyranny.

Regarding the process of amendment prescribed by our Constitution, George Washington wrote, "If in the opinion of the people the distribution or modification of the constitutional powers be in any particular wrong, let it be corrected by an amendment in the way which the Constitution designates, but let there be no change by usurpation; for though this in one instance may be the instrument of good, it is the customary weapon by which free governments are destroyed."

Alexander Hamilton concurred, "[T]he present Constitution is the standard to which we are to cling. Under its banners, bona fide must we combat our political foes – rejecting all changes but through the channel itself provides for amendments."

On the subject of constitutional interpretation, Jefferson wrote: "The Constitution on which our Union rests, shall be administered...according to the safe and honest meaning contemplated by the plain understanding of the people of the United States at the time of its adoption – a meaning to be found in the explanations of those who advocated it. ... On every question of construction, carry ourselves back to the time when the Constitution was adopted, recollect the spirit manifested in the debates and instead of trying what meaning may be squeezed out of the text or invented against it, conform to the probable one in which it was passed. ... Our peculiar security is in the possession of a written Constitution. Let us not make it a blank paper by construction."

James Madison agreed: "I entirely concur in the propriety of resorting to the sense in which the Constitution was accepted and ratified by the nation. In that sense alone it is the legitimate Constitution. And if that is not the guide in expounding it, there may be no security for a consistent and stable, more than for a faithful exercise of its powers."

Justice James Wilson, a signer of the Declaration of Independence and one of the six original Supreme Court justices appointed by George Washington, wrote, "The first and governing maxim in the interpretation of a statute is to discover the meaning of those who made it."

The Federalist Papers, the definitive explication of our Constitution's original intent, clearly delineate constitutional interpretation. In Federalist No. 78 Alexander Hamilton wrote, "[The Judicial Branch] may truly be said to have neither FORCE nor WILL, but merely judgment. ... Liberty can have nothing to fear from the judiciary alone, but would have everything to fear from its union with either of the other departments."

In Federalist No. 81, Hamilton declared, "[T]here is not a syllable in the [Constitution] which directly empowers the national courts to construe the laws according to the spirit of the Constitution. ... [T]he Constitution ought to be the standard of construction for the laws, and that wherever there is an evident opposition, the laws ought to give place to the Constitution." And yet this non-existent "spirit" is the essence of the so-called "living constitution," which liberal jurists now amend by judicial diktat rather than its prescribed method in Article V.

With concern for the future of constitutional integrity, George Washington advised, "The basis of our political systems is the right of the people to make and to alter their Constitutions of Government. But the Constitution which at any time exists, 'till changed by an explicit and authentic act of the whole People is sacredly obligatory upon all."

A "Living Constitution"?

The first instance of extra-constitutional interpretation by the federal judiciary was the 1803 case of Marbury v. Madison. The Supreme Court, under Chief Justice John Marshall, denied the plaintiff's claim because it relied on the Judiciary Act of 1789, which the court ruled unconstitutional.

Marbury set a perilous precedent, but one which would not be used to greatly expand the limited judicial powers outlined in Article III of our Constitution until a century later in a frontal assault on the Rule of Law rivaled only by the constitutional disputes leading to the War Between the States.

Prior to Franklin D. Roosevelt's "New Deal" expansion of central government authority in the 1930s, the courts were still largely populated with originalists, those who properly rendered legal interpretation based on the Constitution's "original intent." But Roosevelt grossly exceeded the constitutional restrictions on his office and that of the legislature in his ill-conceived efforts to end the Great Depression – which ultimately ended during World War II, but not before having long outlasted FDR's social and economic engineering.

So determined was Roosevelt to enact his social welfare policies, that in 1937, he attempted to increase the number of justices on the Supreme Court with the expectation that his appointees would give him a majority and do his political bidding.

It is no coincidence that the term "living constitution" was coined the same year as the title of a book on that subject.

He failed with that approach, but during his unprecedented first three terms, he appointed eight justices to the High Court, who radically accommodated their "interpretation" of the Constitution to conform with Roosevelt's expansion of central government power.

In effect, Roosevelt successfully converted the Judicial Branch from one of independent review according Rule of Law to one of subservience according political will.

In the decades that followed, the notion of a "living constitution," one subject to contemporaneous interpretation informed by political agendas, took hold in federal courts. With increasing frequency, "judicial activists," jurists who "legislate from the bench" by issuing rulings at the behest of like-minded special-interest constituencies, were nominated and confirmed to the Supreme Court.

This degradation in the Rule of Law was codified by the

Warren Court in Trop v. Dulles (1958). In that ruling, the High Court noted that the Constitution should comport with "evolving standards...that mark the progress of a maturing society." In other words, it had now become a fully pliable document, "a mere thing of wax in the hands of the judiciary which they may twist and shape into any form they please," as Thomas Jefferson had warned. Indeed, the Court had mutated into "a despotic branch."

Since then, judicial despots have not only undermined the plain language of our Constitution, but have also grossly devitalized the Bill of Rights.

For example, the First Amendment reads plainly: "Congress shall make no law respecting an establishment of religion, or prohibiting the free exercise thereof; or abridging the freedom of speech, or of the press; or the right of the people peaceably to assemble, and to petition the Government for a redress of grievances."

Once again, in plain language, *"Congress* shall make no law..."

But the courts have ruled this restriction applies to virtually every public forum.

Meanwhile, judicial despots and legislators are endeavoring to supplant authentic freedoms of speech and of press, while asserting that virtually all other mediums of expression constitute "free speech."

As another example, the Second Amendment reads plainly: "A well regulated Militia, being necessary to the security of a free State, the right of the people to keep and bear Arms, shall not be infringed." And yet, certain executive, legislative and judicial principals are unceasing in their efforts to enfeeble this essential right.

During the 1788 Massachusetts Convention debates to ratify the U.S. Constitution, Founder Samuel Adams stated: "The Constitution shall never be construed...to prevent the people of the United States who are peaceable citizens from keeping their own arms."

That same year, James Madison wrote in Federalist No. 46, "The ultimate authority...resides in the people alone. ... The advantage of being armed, which the Americans possess over the people of almost every other nation...forms a barrier against the enterprises of ambition."

In his Commentaries on the Constitution (1833), Justice Joseph Story, appointed to the Supreme Court by James Madison, affirmed the pre-eminence of the Second Amendment: "The right of the citizens to keep and bear arms has justly been considered, as the palladium of the liberties of the republic; since it offers a strong moral check against usurpation and arbitrary power of the rulers, and will generally, even if these are successful in the first instance, enable the people to resist and triumph over them."

Similarly, Founder Noah Webster wrote, "Tyranny is the exercise of some power over a man, which is not warranted by law, or necessary for the public safety. A people can never be deprived of their liberties, while they retain in their own hands, a power sufficient to any other power in the state."

Equally offensive to our Constitution is the manner in which the 10th Amendment's assurance of States' Rights has been eroded by judicial interpretation.

The 10th Amendment reads plainly: "The powers not delegated to the United States by the Constitution, nor prohibited by it to the States, are reserved to the States respectively, or to the people." However, the central government has routinely violated this amendment with all manner of oppressive legislation and regulation over what should be, according to the Rule of Law, matters "reserved to the States respectively, or to the people."

But by the 1980s, judges had become the final arbiter of our Constitution, and its adulteration was so commonplace that liberal Supreme Court Justice Thurgood Marshall was brazenly lecturing on "The Constitution: A Living Document," in defense of constitutional interpretation based upon contemporaneous moral, political and cultural circumstances.

More recently, Justice Antonin Scalia writes, "[There's] the argument of flexibility and it goes something like this: The Constitution is over 200 years old and societies change. It has to change with society, like a living organism, or it will become brittle and break. But you would have to be an idiot to believe that; the Constitution is not a living organism; it is a legal document. It says something and doesn't say other things."

Justice Clarence Thomas follows, "[T]here are really only two ways to interpret the Constitution – try to discern as best we can what the framers intended or make it up. No matter how ingenious, imaginative or artfully put, unless interpretive methodologies are tied to the original intent of the framers, they have no basis in the Constitution. ... To be sure, even the most conscientious effort to adhere to the original intent of the framers of our Constitution is flawed, as all methodologies and human institutions are; but at least originalism has the advantage of being legitimate and, I might add, impartial."

On the political consequences of a "living constitution," Justice Scalia concludes plainly, "If you think aficionados of a living constitution want to bring you flexibility, think again. ... As long as judges tinker with the Constitution to 'do what the people want,' instead of what the document actually commands, politicians who pick and confirm new federal judges will naturally want only those who agree with them politically."

A "Wall of Separation"?

There is no more ominous defilement of our Constitution than that of the errant notion of a "Wall of Separation" between our constitutional government and our Creator – ominous because if the knowledge of our Creator (at one time proliferate in every educational institution) is constrained, then the general knowledge that liberty is "endowed by [our] Creator" will be equally diminished.

As noted in the previous section, our Founders' intent was that the Central government would not appoint any state church by act of Congress. "Congress shall make no law..."

But judicial activists have for decades "interpreted" this First Amendment to suit their political agendas, placing severe constraints upon the free exercise of religion and invoking the obscure and grotesquely misrepresented "Wall of Separation" to expel religious practice from any and all public forums.

As noted by the late Chief Justice of the Supreme Court William Rehnquist, "The wall of separation between church and state is a metaphor based upon bad history, a metaphor which has proved useless as a guide to judging. It should be frankly and explicitly abandoned. ... The greatest injury of the 'wall' notion is its mischievous diversion of judges from the actual intention of the drafters of the Bill of Rights."

George Washington wrote in his 1796 Farewell Address, "Let it simply be asked where is the security for property, for reputation, for life, if the sense of religious obligation deserts the oaths, which are the instruments of investigation in the Courts of Justice? And let us with caution indulge the supposition, that morality can be maintained without religion. Whatever may be conceded to the influence of refined education on minds of peculiar structure, reason and experience both forbid us to expect that National morality can prevail in exclusion of religious principle."

Our Founders affirmed that the natural rights enumerated in our Declaration of Independence and, by extension, as codified in its subordinate guidance, our Constitution, are those endowed by our Creator.

Thomas Jefferson proclaimed, "The God who gave us life, gave us liberty at the same time. ... Can the liberties of a nation be thought secure when we have removed their only firm basis, a conviction in the minds of the people that these liberties are the gift of God? That they are not to be violated but with his wrath? Indeed I tremble for my country when I reflect that God is just: that his justice cannot sleep for ever."

Alexander Hamilton insisted, "The sacred rights of mankind are not to be rummaged for, among old parchments, or musty records. They are written, as with a sun beam, in the whole volume of human nature, by the hand of the divinity itself; and can never be erased or obscured by mortal power."

"Life, liberty and the pursuit of happiness..." These are natural rights – *gifts from God*, not government.

Moreover, it was with firm regard to this fact that our Constitution was written and ratified "in order to secure the Blessings of Liberty to ourselves and our Posterity." As such, it established a constitutional republic ruled by laws based on natural rights, not rights allocated by governments or those occupying seats of power.

John Quincy Adams wrote, "Our political way of life is by the Laws of Nature and of Nature's God, and of course presupposes the existence of God, the moral ruler of the universe, and a rule of right and wrong, of just and unjust, binding upon man, preceding all institutions of human society and government."

Notably, the conviction that our rights are innately bestowed by "the Laws of Nature and of Nature's God," is enumerated in the constitutional preambles of every state in our Union.

But, for many decades, those who advocate a "living constitution" have used the "despotic branch" to remove faith from every public quarter, ironically and erroneously citing the "Wall of Separation" metaphor – words that Jefferson wrote to denote the barrier between federal and state governments, not to erect a prohibition against faith expression in any and all public venues.

The intended consequence of this artificial barrier between church and state is to remove the unmistakable influence of our Creator from all public forums, particularly government education institutions, and thus, over time, to disabuse belief in a sovereign God and the notion of natural rights. This erosion of knowledge about the origin of our rights, the very foundation of our country and basis of our Constitution, has dire implications for the future of liberty.

~~~

"A republic, if you can keep it"

At the close of the Constitution Convention in Philadelphia, Benjamin Franklin was asked if the delegates had formed a republic or a monarchy. "A republic," he responded, "if you can keep it."

He added, "Our new Constitution is now established, and has an appearance that promises permanency; but in this world nothing can be said to be certain, except death and taxes."

To that end, as a warning for future generations to beware of "cunning, ambitious and unprincipled men," George Washington wrote, "A just estimate of that love of power, and proneness to abuse it, which predominates in the human heart is sufficient to satisfy us of the truth of this position."

Daniel Webster wrote, "Good intentions will always be pleaded for every assumption of authority. It is hardly too strong to say that the Constitution was made to guard the people against the dangers of good intentions. There are men in all ages who mean to govern well, but they mean to govern. They promise to be good masters, but they mean to be masters."

Ominously, Alexander Hamilton noted, "Of those men who have overturned the liberties of republics, the greatest number have begun their career by paying an obsequious court to the people, commencing demagogues and ending tyrants."

John Adams observed, "Is the present state of the national republic enough? Is virtue the principle of our government? Is honor? Or is ambition and avarice, adulation, baseness, covetousness, the thirst for riches, indifference concerning the means of rising and enriching, the contempt of principle, the spirit of party and of faction the motive and principle that governs?"

Adams cautioned, "A Constitution of Government once changed from Freedom, can never be restored. Liberty, once lost, is lost forever."

Unfortunately, and at great peril to our liberty, our Constitution has suffered generations of "cunning, ambitious and unprincipled" politicians and judges whose successors now recognize only vestiges of its original intent for governance. Consequently, constitutional Rule of Law has been undermined by those who have deserted their sacred oaths to "support and defend" the same.

As the erosion of constitutional authority undermines individual liberty, it likewise undermines economic liberty.

In Federalist No. 45, James Madison wrote, "The powers delegated by the proposed Constitution to the federal government are few and defined [and] will be exercised principally on external objects, as war, peace, negotiation and foreign commerce."

But by 1794, Madison had begun to rail against government's unconstitutional urge to redistribute the wealth of its citizens: "If Congress can do whatever in their discretion can be done by money, and will promote the General Welfare, the Government is no longer a limited one, possessing enumerated powers, but an indefinite one, subject to particular exceptions."

Jefferson wrote: "[G]iving [Congress] a distinct and independent power to do any act they please which may be good for the Union, would render all the preceding and subsequent enumerations of power completely useless. It would reduce the whole [Constitution] to a single phrase, that of instituting a Congress with power to do whatever would be for the good of the United States; and as sole judges of the good or evil, it would be also a power to do whatever evil they please. Certainly no such universal power was meant to be given them. [The Constitution] was intended to lace them up straightly within the enumerated powers and those without which, as means, these powers could not be carried into effect."

But at the onset of the Great Depression a century later, that same wealthy aristocrat, Franklin Roosevelt, who up-ended constitutionally limited government, undertook an equally injurious assault on economic liberty.

FDR, like many "inheritance welfare" politicos today, had an unquenchable thirst for power and used the Great Depression as cover to redefine and expand the role of the central government via countless extra-constitutional decrees as well as the means to justify how the government would fund that folly.

Roosevelt issued this dubious proclamation: "Here is my principle: Taxes shall be levied according to ability to pay. That is the only American principle."

Of course, his "American principle" was nothing more than a paraphrase of Karl Marx's maxim, "From each according to his abilities, to each according to his needs."

Indeed, Roosevelt's "principles" had no basis in the Rule of Law or the laws of free enterprise, and his New Deal gave rise to what is now the central government's most oppressive weapon: The U.S. Tax Code.

Of government welfare programs, Madison wrote, "I cannot undertake to lay my finger on that article of the Constitution which granted a right to Congress of expending, on objects of benevolence, the money of their constituents..."

Accordingly, Article 1, Section 8 of our Constitution, which addresses the powers of the legislature, does not give Congress the authority to collect taxes for banking, mortgage and automaker bailouts, or to subsidize production or service sectors like healthcare, or to fund education and retirement, much less, tens-of-thousands of earmarks for special interest "pork projects."

Congress is also not authorized to institute countless conditions for the redistribution of wealth in its 20 volume, 14,000 page Tax Code, or to impose millions of regulations on everything from CO_2 emissions to toilet water volume.

Today, more than 70 percent of the federal budget is spent on "objects of benevolence," for which there is no constitutional authority. Put another way, much of your income is confiscated by the government and redistributed unconstitutionally. And the current Democrat hegemony has saddled the nation with more government debt than all previous administrations combined, in effect assuring the confiscation of income from future generations for purposes not expressly authorized by our Constitution.

Of such debt, Jefferson concluded, "The principle of spending money to be paid by posterity, under the name of funding, is but swindling futurity on a large scale."

Principium Imprimis

"In disquisitions of every kind there are certain primary

truths, or first principles, upon which all subsequent reasoning must depend." –Alexander Hamilton

If there is to be a peaceful transfer of liberty to our posterity, then we must return to *principium imprimis*, or First Principles.

Short of another American Revolution to remove by force those in government who do not abide by their oaths "to support and defend the Constitution of the United States against all enemies, foreign and domestic," our freedoms cannot long endure unless we, the people, reaffirm what was well understood by our Founders: that our Creator is the only eternal assurance of liberty.

The primacy of faith must be restored in order to preserve the conviction that, as Jefferson wrote, our "liberties are the gift of God"; traditional families and values must be restored as the foundation of our culture; individual rights and responsibilities must be restored as the underpinning of republican government; free enterprise must be unbridled from government constraints; and constitutional authority over each branch of government must be restored to ensure liberty, opportunity and prosperity for a civil society.

The Cycle of Democracy has been summarized as: From bondage to spiritual faith; From spiritual faith to great courage; From courage to liberty (rule of law); From liberty to abundance; From abundance to complacency; From complacency to apathy; From apathy to dependence; From dependence back into bondage (rule of men).

Our Founders established a democratic republic, not a democracy, in order to enfeeble this cycle. However, with the erosion of constitutional authority, our Republic is now in grave peril of following the same cycle as have all other democracies in history. Only intervention by citizens and leaders who advocate the primacy of constitutional authority, those committed to supporting and defending that authority above their self-interest, can save the Republic for the next generation.

Irrevocably linked to liberty ensured by constitutional Rule of Law is economic liberty.

In 1916, a minister and outspoken advocate for liberty, William J. H. Boetcker, published a pamphlet entitled The Ten Cannots:

You cannot bring about prosperity by discouraging thrift.

You cannot strengthen the weak by weakening the strong.

You cannot help the poor man by destroying the rich.

You cannot further the brotherhood of man by inciting class hatred.

You cannot build character and courage by taking away man's initiative and independence.

You cannot help small men by tearing down big men.

You cannot lift the wage earner by pulling down the wage payer.

You cannot keep out of trouble by spending more than your income.

You cannot establish security on borrowed money.

You cannot help men permanently by doing for them what they will not do for themselves.

Fact is, the central government cannot give to anybody what it does not first take from somebody else.

So what is a Patriot to do?

Some of our countrymen are overwhelmed with the current state of affairs. They have resigned to defeat and with-drawn from the fields of battle. In so doing, they betray the legacy of liberty extended to them by generations of Patriots who have pledged their "Lives, Fortunes and Sacred Honor."

Of such resignation, Hamilton wrote, "A nation which can prefer disgrace to danger is prepared for a master, and deserves one!"

Franklin insisted, "They that can give up essential liberty to obtain a little temporary safety deserve neither liberty nor safety."

Samuel Adams showed no sympathy for such retreat: "Contemplate the mangled bodies of your countrymen, and then say 'what should be the reward of such sacrifices?' ... If ye love wealth better than liberty, the tranquility of servitude than the animated contest of freedom, go from us in peace. We ask not your counsels or arms. Crouch down and lick the hands which feed you. May your chains sit lightly upon you, and may posterity forget that you were our countrymen!"

Patrick Henry said famously, "Is life so dear or peace so sweet as to be purchased at the price of chains and slavery? Forbid it, Almighty God! I know not what course others may take, but as for me, give me liberty or give me death!"

Plainly, none can claim the name "American Patriot" if they submit to laws and regulations, which violate the most fundamental tenets of our Constitution.

At its core, the word "patriot" has direct lineage to those who fought for American independence and established our constitutional Republic. That lineage has descended through our history most conspicuously by way of those who have pledged "to support and defend" our Constitution – those who have been faithful to and have abided by their oaths, even unto death.

Today, those who can rightly claim the name Patriot, those who have stood firm on the front lines of the struggle to restore constitutional integrity, be encouraged. There is a groundswell of activism across the Fruited Plain, as our fellow countrymen are awakening to the ominous threat of constitutional adulteration and its irrevocable terminus: tyranny.

The growing chorus of Patriot voices from every corner of the nation and all walks of life is demanding restoration of the Rule of Law as outlined by our Constitution.

Today's Patriots exemplify not only the eternal spirit of liberty conferred through the ages by previous generations of Patriots, but also a spirit enlivened in recent history by a conservative who spent much of his life as a Democrat (even heading a major union at one time).

That man became an outspoken conservative in reaction to the Democrat Party's increasing betrayal of our Constitution, declaring, "I didn't leave the Democratic Party; the Democratic Party left me."

He was elected president in 1980 on a platform of constitutional integrity and federalism, and he was devoted to that doctrine. He was re-elected on those principles four years later in a landslide victory – winning every state but his opponent's home state (and, of course, the District of Columbia).

His name was Ronald Wilson Reagan, and he delivered a treatise on liberty in 1964, "A Time for Choosing," which to this day appositely frames conservative philosophy.

In "The Speech," as we know it, Reagan insisted, "I think it's time we ask ourselves if we still know the freedoms that were intended for us by the Founding Fathers. ... Whether we believe in our capacity for self-government or whether we abandon the American Revolution and confess that a little intellectual elite in a far-distant capital can plan our lives for us better than we can plan them ourselves."

He continued: "You and I are told increasingly that we have to choose between a left or right, but I would like to suggest that there is no such thing as a left or right. There is only an up or down – up to a man's age-old dream; the ultimate in individual freedom consistent with law and order – or down to the ant heap of totalitarianism, and regardless of their sincerity, their humanitarian motives, those who would trade our freedom for security have embarked on this downward course."

Some said President Reagan won broad support because he was a "great communicator," but he said more accurately in his farewell address: "I wasn't a great communicator, but I communicated great things, and they didn't spring full bloom from my brow, they came from the heart of a great nation – from our experience, our wisdom, and our belief in principles that have guided us for two centuries."

The principles of liberty advanced by President Reagan were, and remain, a template for victory over tyranny. But our legacy of liberty is at grave risk today. Indeed, we face another time for choosing.

While the words "conservative" and "liberal" are ubiquitously used to describe party alliances, these words more essentially describe whether one advocates the Rule of Law, or the rule of men; for the conservation of our Constitution as the Founders intended, or its liberal interpretation by "progressive" legislators and judicial activists.

It is time for each of us to choose which we advocate and to fully understand the consequences of that choice.

It is time for those of us who endorse the most basic tenets of our Republic, "That all men are created equal, that they are endowed by their Creator with certain unalienable Rights, that among these are Life, Liberty and the pursuit of Happiness," to honor that heritage and set about the formidable task of restoring individual liberty and constitutional limits upon the branches of our national government.

The futility of debating policy matters must now yield to a more substantive national debate about constitutional authority.

The time is at hand when we must inquire with a unified voice: "If there is no constitutional authority for laws and regulations enacted by Congress and enforced by the central government, then by what authority do those entities lay and collect taxes to fund such laws and regulations?"

On July 4th, 1776, our Declaration of Independence, this nation's supreme manuscript of incorporation, asserted, "That whenever any Form of Government becomes destructive of these ends, it is the Right of the People to alter or to abolish it, and to institute new Government..."

Our Declaration's principal author, Thomas Jefferson, also wrote, "The tree of liberty must be refreshed from time to time with the blood of patriots and tyrants. ... Resistance to tyrants is obedience to God."

While one prays that liberty will be restored and extended to *our* posterity without spirited rebellion, history does not favor such prospects.

At present, our Constitution is in virtual exile, and the central government is in the hands of those who believe they are the arbiters of liberty, rather than its endowment by our Creator.

It is time for tenacious resistance and rebellion against the current thrones of government. This is not a call for revolution but for restoration – to undertake whatever measures are dictated by prudence and necessity to restore constitutional Rule of Law.

Ronald Reagan said, "There are no easy answers, but there are simple answers. We must have the courage to do what we know is morally right. ... You and I have a rendezvous with destiny. We will preserve for our children this, the last best hope of man on earth, or we will sentence them to take the last step into a thousand years of darkness."

Which will it be?

Fellow Patriots, I implore you to make no peace with oppression, and I leave you with these words of encouragement from the Father of our Nation, George Washington: "We should never despair. Our situation before has been unpromising and has changed for the better, so I trust, it will again. If new difficulties arise, we must only put forth new exertions and proportion our efforts to the exigency of the times."

Semper Vigilo, Fortis, Paratus et Fidelis!

Mark Alexander
Publisher, *The Patriot Post* – PatriotPost.US
Founder, *Essential Liberty Project* – EssentialLibertyProject.US

ABOUT THE OATH
TO SUPPORT AND DEFEND

"Let it simply be asked where is the security for property, for reputation, for life, if the sense of religious obligation deserts the oaths... ?" – George Washington

The last line of our Declaration of Independence reads, "For the support of this declaration, with a firm reliance on the protection of Divine Providence, we mutually pledge to each other our lives, our fortunes and our sacred honor."

Indeed, many first-generation American Patriots died fighting for American liberty.

A decade later, their liberty won at great cost, our Founders further codified their independence and interdependence by instituting our Constitution, which specifies in Article VI, clause 3:

"The Senators and Representatives before mentioned, and the Members of the several State Legislatures, and all executive and judicial Officers, both of the United States and of the several States, shall be bound by Oath [emphasis added] or Affirmation, to support this Constitution..."

The Constitution prescribed the following oath to be taken by the president-elect: "I do solemnly swear that I will faithfully execute the office of President of the United States, and will to the best of my ability, preserve, protect and defend [emphasis added] the Constitution of the United States."

Regarding the Presidential Oath of Office, Justice Joseph Story wrote: "[T]he duty imposed upon him to take care, that the laws be faithfully executed, follows out the strong injunctions of his oath of office, that he will 'preserve, protect, and defend the Constitution.' The great object of the executive department is to accomplish this purpose." Story wrote further that if the president does not honor his oath, his office "will be utterly worthless for...the protection of rights; for the happiness, or good order, or safety of the people."

Members of Congress and commissioned military personnel are also required by statute to "solemnly swear, that I will support and defend the Constitution of the United States against all enemies, foreign and domestic [emphasis added]: that I will bear true faith and allegiance to the same, that I take this obligation freely, without any mental reservation or purpose of evasion; and that I will well and faithfully discharge the duties of the office on which I am about to enter: So help me God."

The oath for enlisted military personnel repeats the preceding affirmation, "that I will support and defend the Constitution of the United States against all enemies, foreign and domestic; that I will bear true faith and allegiance to the same," and concludes with, "I will obey the orders of the President of the United States and the orders of the officers appointed over me, according to regulations and the Uniform Code of Military Justice. So help me God."

The subtle distinction between officer oath and enlisted oath is that officers are bound to disobey any order that violates our Constitution, while enlisted personnel are bound to obey only lawful orders.

Similar oaths are taken by state and local elected representatives, and federal, state and local civil servants.

Notably, these oaths mandate the preservation, protection, support and defense of our Constitution as ratified, not a so-called "living constitution." And by extension, every American Patriot who has taken such an oath is bound by his or her pledge to also support and defend the Constitution's foundation, the Declaration of Independence, and the Declaration's basis, Natural Law.

While uniformed Americans serving our nation defend our Constitution with their lives, many elected officials debase it by enacting extra-constitutional empowerments of the central government, invariably to appease special constituencies and/or to perpetuate their office.

Although military service personnel who violate their oaths are remanded for courts-martial under the Uniform Code of Military Justice, politicians who violate their oaths are often rewarded with re-election. However, those who do not abide by their oaths, elected officials first and foremost among them, must rightly and justly be removed from office, posthaste, and prosecuted to the fullest extent of the law.

On the following page, you will have the opportunity to affirm or reaffirm your oath to "support and defend the Constitution of the United States against all enemies, foreign and domestic..."

Generations of American Patriots have sacrificed their lives in defense of our Constitution. Do not undertake to affirm your oath to the same unless you are prepared to support and defend it with your life, your fortune and your sacred honor.

Affirm or Reaffirm Your Oath

With a full understanding of the authority of the United States Constitution and the Rule of Law, reaffirm your oath to "support and defend" our Constitution "against all enemies, foreign and domestic."

If you have previously taken an oath to our Constitution and you remain steadfast in your pledge to "bear true faith and allegiance to the same," please affirm this by your signature:

_____ *Signature*

Oath taken as Military
☐ *Officer* or ☐ *Enlisted*

Oath taken as Civilian
☐ *Elected* or ☐ *Civil Servant* or ☐ *Public Servant*

Year of Initial Oath: _____

Having reaffirmed your oath, please administer it to those who have not, and stand ready to abide by it when duty calls.

If you are among those who have not yet taken the oath to support and defend, request its administration from a fellow Patriot who has so you can administer it to those who have not, and stand ready to abide by it when duty calls.

OATH OF ALLEGIANCE
TO SUPPORT AND DEFEND
THE UNITED STATES
CONSTITUTION

I, _____ (Printed Name)
do solemnly swear, that I will support and defend the
Constitution of the United States against all enemies, foreign
and domestic: that I will bear true faith and allegiance to the
same, that I take this obligation freely, without any mental
reservation or purpose of evasion; and that I will well and
faithfully discharge the duties of the office on which I am
about to enter: So help me God."

_____ *Signature*

Administered by: _____

Affirmed on this ____ *Day of* _____ *in the Year* _____

Essential Liberty Online
*For additional resources, join the ranks of other Patriots who have
registered their oath online in our state-by-state registry.
Link to the Oath page at ToSupportandDefend.US*

DECLARATION OF
THE CAUSE AND NECESSITY
OF TAKING UP ARMS

July 6, 1775

A declaration by the representatives of the united colonies of North America, now met in Congress at Philadelphia, setting forth the causes and necessity of their taking up arms.

If it was possible for men, who exercise their reason to believe, that the divine Author of our existence intended a part of the human race to hold an absolute property in, and an unbounded power over others, marked out by his infinite goodness and wisdom, as the objects of a legal domination never rightfully resistible, however severe and oppressive, the inhabitants of these colonies might at least require from the parliament of Great-Britain some evidence, that this dreadful authority over them, has been granted to that body. But a reverance for our Creator, principles of humanity, and the dictates of common sense, must convince all those who reflect upon the subject, that government was instituted to promote the welfare of mankind, and ought to be administered for the attainment of that end. The legislature of Great-Britain, however, stimulated by an inordinate passion for a power not only unjustifiable, but which they know to be peculiarly reprobated by the very constitution of that kingdom, and desparate of success in any mode of contest, where regard should be had to truth, law, or right, have at length, deserting those, attempted to effect their cruel and impolitic purpose of enslaving these colonies by violence, and have thereby rendered it necessary for us to close with their last appeal from reason to arms. Yet, however blinded that assembly may be, by their intemperate rage for unlimited domination, so to sight justice and the opinion of mankind, we esteem ourselves bound by obligations of respect to the rest of the world, to make known the justice of our cause. Our forefathers, inhabitants of the island of Great-Britain, left their native land, to seek on these shores a residence for civil and religious freedom. At the expense of their blood, at the hazard of their fortunes, without the least charge to the country from which they removed, by unceasing labour, and an unconquerable spirit, they effected settlements in the distant and unhospitable wilds of America, then filled with numerous and warlike barbarians. – Societies or governments, vested with perfect legislatures, were formed under charters from the crown, and an harmonious intercourse was established between the colonies and the kingdom from which they derived their origin. The mutual benefits of this union became in a short time so extraordinary, as to excite astonishment. It is universally confessed, that the amazing increase of the wealth, strength, and navigation of the realm, arose from this source; and the minister, who so wisely and successfully directed the measures of Great-Britain in the late war, publicly declared, that these colonies enabled her to triumph over her enemies. –Towards the conclusion of that war, it pleased our sovereign to make a change in his counsels. – From that fatal movement, the affairs of the British empire began to fall into confusion, and gradually sliding from the summit of glorious prosperity, to which they had been advanced by the virtues and abilities of one man, are at length distracted by the convulsions, that now shake it to its deepest foundations. – The new ministry finding the brave foes of Britain, though frequently defeated, yet still contending, took up the unfortunate idea of granting them a hasty peace, and then subduing her faithful friends.

These colonies were judged to be in such a state, as to present victories without bloodshed, and all the easy emoluments of statuteable plunder. – The uninterrupted tenor of their peaceable and respectful behaviour from the beginning of colonization, their dutiful, zealous, and useful services during the war, though so recently and amply acknowledged in the most honourable manner by his majesty, by the late king, and by parliament, could not save them from the meditated innovations. – Parliament was influenced to adopt the pernicious project, and assuming a new power over them, have in the course of eleven years, given such decisive specimens of the spirit and consequences attending this power, as to leave no doubt concerning the effects of acquiescence under it. They have undertaken to give and grant our money without our consent, though we have ever exercised an exclusive right to dispose of our own property; statutes have been passed for extending the jurisdiction of courts of admiralty and vice-admiralty beyond their ancient limits; for depriving

us of the accustomed and inestimable privilege of trial by
jury, in cases affecting both life and property; for suspending the legislature of one of the colonies; for interdicting
all commerce to the capital of another; and for altering
fundamentally the form of government established by
charter, and secured by acts of its own legislature solemnly
confirmed by the crown; for exempting the "murderers" of
colonists from legal trial, and in effect, from punishment;
for erecting in a neighbouring province, acquired by the
joint arms of Great-Britain and America, a despotism dangerous to our very existence; and for quartering soldiers
upon the colonists in time of profound peace. It has also
been resolved in parliament, that colonists charged with
committing certain offences, shall be transported to Eng
land to be tried. But why should we enumerate our injuries
in detail? By one statute it is declared, that parliament can
"of right make laws to bind us in all cases whatsoever."
What is to defend us against so enormous, so unlimited a
power? Not a single man of those who assume it, is chosen
by us; or is subject to our control or influence; but, on the
contrary, they are all of them exempt from the operation
of such laws, and an American revenue, if not diverted
from the ostensible purposes for which it is raised, would
actually lighten their own burdens in proportion, as they
increase ours. We saw the misery to which such despotism
would reduce us. We for ten years incessantly and inef-
fectually besieged the throne as supplicants; we reasoned,
we remonstrated with parliament, in the most mild and
decent language.

Administration sensible that we should regard these oppressive measures as freemen ought to do, sent over fleets and armies to enforce them. The indignation of the Americans was roused, it is true; but it was the indignation of a virtuous, loyal, and affectionate people. A Congress of delegates from the United Colonies was assembled at Philadelphia, on the fifth day of last September. We resolved again to offer an humble and dutiful petition to the King, and also addressed our fellow-subjects of Great-Britain. We have pursued every temperate, every respectful measure; we have even proceeded to break off our commercial intercourse with our fellow-subjects, as the last peaceable admonition, that our attachment to no nation upon earth should supplant our attachment to liberty. – This, we flattered ourselves, was the ultimate step of the controversy: but subsequent events have shewn, how vain was this hope of finding moderation in our enemies.

Several threatening expressions against the colonies were inserted in his majesty's speech; our petition, tho' we were told it was a decent one, and that his majesty had been pleased to receive it graciously, and to promise laying it before his parliament, was huddled into both houses among a bundle of American papers, and there neglected. The lords and commons in their address, in the month of February, said, that "a rebellion at that time actually existed within the province of Massachusetts- Bay; and that those concerned with it, had been countenanced and encouraged by unlawful combinations and engagements, entered into by his majesty's subjects in several of the other colonies;

and therefore they besought his majesty, that he would take the most effectual measures to inforce due obediance to the laws and authority of the supreme legislature." – Soon after, the commercial intercourse of whole colonies, with foreign countries, and with each other, was cut off by an act of parliament; by another several of them were intirely prohibited from the fisheries in the seas near their coasts, on which they always depended for their sustenance; and large reinforcements of ships and troops were immediately sent over to general Gage.

Fruitless were all the entreaties, arguments, and eloquence of an illustrious band of the most distinguished peers, and commoners, who nobly and strenuously asserted the justice of our cause, to stay, or even to mitigate the heedless fury with which these accumulated and unexampled outrages were hurried on. – equally fruitless was the interference of the city of London, of Bristol, and many other respectable towns in our favor. Parliament adopted an insidious manoeuvre calculated to divide us, to establish a perpetual auction of taxations where colony should bid against colony, all of them uninformed what ransom would redeem their lives; and thus to extort from us, at the point of the bayonet, the unknown sums that should be sufficient to gratify, if possible to gratify, ministerial rapacity, with the miserable indulgence left to us of raising, in our own mode, the prescribed tribute. What terms more rigid and humiliating could have been dictated by remorseless victors to conquered enemies? in our circumstances to accept them, would be to deserve them.

Soon after the intelligence of these proceedings arrived on this continent, general Gage, who in the course of the last year had taken possession of the town of Boston, in the province of Massachusetts-Bay, and still occupied it a garrison, on the 19th day of April, sent out from that place a large detachment of his army, who made an unprovoked assault on the inhabitants of the said province, at the town of Lexington, as appears by the affidavits of a great number of persons, some of whom were officers and soldiers of that detachment, murdered eight of the inhabitants, and wounded many others. From thence the troops proceeded in warlike array to the town of Concord, where they set upon another party of the inhabitants of the same province, killing several and wounding more, until compelled to retreat by the country people suddenly assembled to repel this cruel aggression. Hostilities, thus commenced by the British troops, have been since prosecuted by them without regard to faith or reputation. – The inhabitants of Boston being confined within that town by the general their governor, and having, in order to procure their dismission, entered into a treaty with him, it was stipulated that the said inhabitants having deposited their arms with their own magistrate, should have liberty to depart, taking with them their other effects. They accordingly delivered up their arms, but in open violation of honour, in defiance of the obligation of treaties, which even savage nations esteemed sacred, the governor ordered the arms deposited as aforesaid, that they might be preserved for their owners, to be seized by a body of soldiers; detained the greatest part of the inhabitants in the town, and compelled the few who were permitted to retire, to leave their most valuable effects behind.

By this perfidy wives are separated from their husbands, children from their parents, the aged and the sick from their relations and friends, who wish to attend and comfort them; and those who have been used to live in plenty and even elegance, are reduced to deplorable distress.

The general, further emulating his ministerial masters, by a proclamation bearing date on the 12th day of June, after venting the grossest falsehoods and calumnies against the good people of these colonies, proceeds to "declare them all, either by name or description, to be rebels and traitors, to supercede the course of the common law, and instead thereof to publish and order the use and exercise of the law martial." – His troops have butchered our country-men, have wantonly burnt Charlestown, besides a considerable number of houses in other places; our ships and vessels are seized; the necessary supplies of provisions are intercepted, and he is exerting his utmost power to spread destruction and devastation around him.

We have received certain intelligence, that general Carleton, the governor of Canada, is instigating the people of that province and the Indians to fall upon us; and we have but too much reason to apprehend, that schemes have been formed to excite domestic enemies against us. In brief, a part of these colonies now feel, and all of them are sure of feeling, as far as the vengeance of administration can inflict them, the complicated calamities of fire, sword and famine.

We are reduced to the alternative of chusing an unconditional submission to the tyranny of irritated ministers, or resistance by force. – The latter is our choice. – We have counted the cost of this contest, and find nothing so dreadful as voluntary slavery. – Honour, justice, and humanity, forbid us tamely to surrender that freedom which we received from our gallant ancestors, and which our innocent posterity have a right to receive from us. We cannot endure the infamy and guilt of resigning succeeding generations to that wretchedness which inevitably awaits them, if we basely entail hereditary bondage upon them.

Our cause is just. Our union is perfect. Our internal resources are great, and, if necessary, foreign assistance is undoubtedly attainable. – We gratefully acknowledge, as signal instances of the Divine favour towards us, that his Providence would not permit us to be called into this severe controversy, until we were grown up to our present strength, had been previously exercised in warlike operation, and possessed of the means of defending ourselves. With hearts fortified with these animating reflections, we most solemnly, before God and the world, declare, that, exerting the utmost energy of those powers, which our beneficent Creator hath graciously bestowed upon us, the arms we have been compelled by our enemies to assume, we will, in defiance of every hazard, with unabating firmness and perseverence, employ for the preservation of our liberties; being with one mind resolved to die freemen rather than to live slaves.

Lest this declaration should disquiet the minds of our

friends and fellow-subjects in any part of the empire, we assure them that we mean not to dissolve that union which has so long and so happily subsisted between us, and which we sincerely wish to see restored. – Necessity has not yet driven us into that desperate measure, or induced us to excite any other nation to war against them. – We have not raised armies with ambitious designs of separating from Great-Britain, and establishing independent states. We fight not for glory or for conquest. We exhibit to mankind the remarkable spectacle of a people attacked by unprovoked enemies, without any imputation or even suspicion of offence. They boast of their privileges and civilization, and yet proffer no milder conditions than servitude or death.

In our own native land, in defence of the freedom that is our birthright, and which we ever enjoyed till the late violation of it – for the protection of our property, acquired solely by the honest industry of our fore-fathers and ourselves, against violence actually offered, we have taken up arms. We shall lay them down when hostilities shall cease on the part of the aggressors, and all danger of their being renewed shall be removed, and not before.

With an humble confidence in the mercies of the supreme and impartial Judge and Ruler of the Universe, we most devoutly implore his divine goodness to protect us happily through this great conflict, to dispose our adversaries to reconciliation on reasonable terms, and thereby to relieve the empire from the calamities of civil war.

THE VIRGINIA DECLARATION OF RIGHTS

June 12, 1776

1. That all men are by nature equally free and independent, and have certain inherent rights, of which, when they enter into a state of society, they cannot, by any compact, deprive or divest their posterity; namely, the enjoyment of life and liberty, with the means of acquiring and possessing property, and pursuing and obtaining happiness and safety.

2. That all power is vested in, and consequently derived from, the people; that magistrates are their trustees and servants, and at all times amenable to them.

3. That government is, or ought to be, instituted for the common benefit, protection, and security of the people, nation or community; of all the various modes and forms of government that is best, which is capable of producing the greatest degree of happiness and safety and is most effectually secured against the danger of maladministration; and that, whenever any government shall be found inadequate or contrary to these purposes, a majority of the community hath an indubitable, unalienable, and indefeasible right to reform, alter or abolish it, in such manner as shall be judged most conducive to the public weal.

4. That no man, or set of men, are entitled to exclusive or separate emoluments or privileges from the community, but in consideration of public services; which, not being descendible, neither ought the offices of magistrate, legislator, or judge be hereditary.

5. That the legislative and executive powers of the state should be separate and distinct from the judicative; and, that the members of the two first may be restrained from oppression by feeling and participating the burthens of the people, they should, at fixed periods, be reduced to a private station, return into that body from which they were originally taken, and the vacancies be supplied by frequent, certain, and regular elections in which all, or any part of the former members, to be again eligible, or ineligible, as the laws shall direct.

6. That elections of members to serve as representatives of the people in assembly ought to be free; and that all men, having sufficient evidence of permanent common interest with, and attachment to, the community have the right of suffrage and cannot be taxed or deprived of their property for public uses without their own consent or that of their representatives so elected, nor bound by any law to which they have not, in like manner, assented, for the public good.

7. That all power of suspending laws, or the execution of laws, by any authority without consent of the representatives of the people is injurious to their rights and ought not to be exercised.

8. That in all capital or criminal prosecutions a man hath a right to demand the cause and nature of his accusation to be confronted with the accusers and witnesses, to call for evidence in his favor, and to a speedy trial by an impartial jury of his vicinage, without whose unanimous consent he cannot be found guilty, nor can he be compelled to give evidence against himself; that no man be deprived of his liberty except by the law of the land or the judgement of his peers.

9. That excessive bail ought not to be required, nor excessive fines imposed; nor cruel and unusual punishments inflicted.

10. That general warrants, whereby any officer or messenger may be commanded to search suspected places without evidence of a fact committed, or to seize any person or persons not named, or whose offense is not particularly described and supported by evidence, are grievous and oppressive and ought not to be granted.

11. That in controversies respecting property and in suits between man and man, the ancient trial by jury is preferable to any other and ought to be held sacred.

12. That the freedom of the press is one of the greatest bulwarks of liberty and can never be restrained but by despotic governments.

13. That a well regulated militia, composed of the body of the people, trained to arms, is the proper, natural, and safe defense of a free state; that standing armies, in time of peace, should be avoided as dangerous to liberty; and that, in all cases, the military should be under strict subordination to, and be governed by, the civil power.

14. That the people have a right to uniform government; and therefore, that no government separate from, or independent of, the government of Virginia, ought to be erected or established within the limits thereof.

15. That no free government, or the blessings of liberty, can be preserved to any people but by a firm adherence to justice, moderation, temperance, frugality, and virtue and by frequent recurrence to fundamental principles.

16. That religion, or the duty which we owe to our Creator and the manner of discharging it, can be directed by reason and conviction, not by force or violence; and therefore, all men are equally entitled to the free exercise of religion, according to the dictates of conscience; and that it is the mutual duty of all to practice Christian forbearance, love, and charity towards each other.

Adopted unanimously June 12, 1776 Virginia Convention of Delegates drafted by Mr. George Mason

The Declaration of Independence

IN CONGRESS, JULY 4, 1776

The unanimous Declaration
of the thirteen united States of America,

When in the Course of human events, it becomes necessary for one people to dissolve the political bands which have connected them with another, and to assume among the powers of the earth, the separate and equal station to which the Laws of Nature and of Nature's God entitle them, a decent respect to the opinions of mankind requires that they should declare the causes which impel them to the separation.

We hold these truths to be self-evident, that all men are created equal, that they are endowed by their Creator with certain unalienable Rights, that among these are Life, Liberty and the pursuit of Happiness.–That to secure these rights, Governments are instituted among Men, deriving their just powers from the consent of the governed, –That whenever any Form of Government becomes destructive of these ends, it is the Right of the People to alter or to abolish it, and to institute new Government, laying its foundation on such principles and organizing its powers in such form, as to them shall seem most likely to effect their Safety and Happiness. Prudence, indeed, will dictate that Governments long established should not be changed for light and transient causes; and accordingly all experience hath shewn, that mankind are more disposed to suffer, while evils are sufferable, than to right themselves by abolishing the forms to which they are accustomed. But when a long train of abuses and usurpations, pursuing invariably the same Object evinces a design to reduce them under absolute Despotism, it is their right, it is their duty, to throw off such Government, and to provide new Guards for their future security.–Such has been the patient sufferance of these Colonies; and such is now the necessity which constrains them to alter their former Systems of Government. The history of the present King of Great Britain is a history of repeated injuries and usurpations, all having in direct object the establishment of an absolute Tyranny over these States. To prove this, let Facts be submitted to a candid world.

He has refused his Assent to Laws, the most wholesome and necessary for the public good.

He has forbidden his Governors to pass Laws of immediate and pressing importance, unless suspended in their operation till his Assent should be obtained; and when so suspended, he has utterly neglected to attend to them.

He has refused to pass other Laws for the accommodation of large districts of people, unless those people would relinquish the right of Representation in the Legislature, a right inestimable to them and formidable to tyrants only.

He has called together legislative bodies at places unusual, uncomfortable, and distant from the depository of their public Records, for the sole purpose of fatiguing them into compliance with his measures.

He has dissolved Representative Houses repeatedly, for

opposing with manly firmness his invasions on the rights of the people.

He has refused for a long time, after such dissolutions, to cause others to be elected; whereby the Legislative powers, incapable of Annihilation, have returned to the People at large for their exercise; the State remaining in the mean time exposed to all the dangers of invasion from without, and convulsions within.

He has endeavoured to prevent the population of these States; for that purpose obstructing the Laws for Naturalization of Foreigners; refusing to pass others to encourage their migrations hither, and raising the conditions of new Appropriations of Lands.

He has obstructed the Administration of Justice, by refusing his Assent to Laws for establishing Judiciary powers.

He has made Judges dependent on his Will alone, for the tenure of their offices, and the amount and payment of their salaries.

He has erected a multitude of New Offices, and sent hither swarms of Officers to harrass our people, and eat out their substance.

He has kept among us, in times of peace, Standing Armies without the Consent of our legislatures.

He has affected to render the Military independent of and superior to the Civil power.

He has combined with others to subject us to a jurisdiction foreign to our constitution, and unacknowledged by our laws; giving his Assent to their Acts of pretended Legislation:

For Quartering large bodies of armed troops among us:

For protecting them, by a mock Trial, from punishment for any Murders which they should commit on the Inhabitants of these States:

For cutting off our Trade with all parts of the world:

For imposing Taxes on us without our Consent:

For depriving us in many cases, of the benefits of Trial by Jury:

For transporting us beyond Seas to be tried for pretended offences:

For abolishing the free System of English Laws in a neighbouring Province, establishing therein an Arbitrary government, and enlarging its Boundaries so as to render it at once an example and fit instrument for introducing the same absolute rule into these Colonies:

For taking away our Charters, abolishing our most valuable Laws, and altering fundamentally the Forms of our Governments:

For suspending our own Legislatures, and declaring themselves invested with power to legislate for us in all cases whatsoever.

He has abdicated Government here, by declaring us out of his Protection and waging War against us.

He has plundered our seas, ravaged our Coasts, burnt our towns, and destroyed the lives of our people.

He is at this time transporting large Armies of foreign Mercenaries to compleat the works of death, desolation and tyranny, already begun with circumstances of Cruelty & perfidy scarcely parallelled in the most barbarous ages, and totally unworthy the Head of a civilized nation.

He has constrained our fellow Citizens taken Captive on the high Seas to bear Arms against their Country, to become the executioners of their friends and Brethren, or to fall themselves by their Hands.

He has excited domestic insurrections amongst us, and has endeavoured to bring on the inhabitants of our frontiers, the merciless Indian Savages, whose known rule of warfare, is an undistinguished destruction of all ages, sexes and conditions.

In every stage of these Oppressions We have Petitioned for Redress in the most humble terms: Our repeated Petitions have been answered only by repeated injury. A Prince whose character is thus marked by every act which may define a Tyrant, is unfit to be the ruler of a free people.

Nor have We been wanting in attentions to our Brittish brethren. We have warned them from time to time of attempts by their legislature to extend an unwarrantable jurisdiction over us. We have reminded them of the circumstances of our emigration and settlement here. We have appealed to their native justice and magnanimity, and we have conjured them by the ties of our common kindred to disavow these usurpations, which, would inevitably interrupt our connections and correspondence. They too have been deaf to the voice of justice and of consanguinity. We must, therefore, acquiesce in the necessity, which denounces our Separation, and hold them, as we hold the rest of mankind, Enemies in War, in Peace Friends.

We, therefore, the Representatives of the united States of America, in General Congress, Assembled, appealing to the

Supreme Judge of the world for the rectitude of our intentions, do, in the Name, and by Authority of the good People of these Colonies, solemnly publish and declare, That these United Colonies are, and of Right ought to be Free and Independent States; that they are Absolved from all Allegiance to the British Crown, and that all political connection between them and the State of Great Britain, is and ought to be totally dissolved; and that as Free and Independent States, they have full Power to levy War, conclude Peace, contract Alliances, establish Commerce, and to do all other Acts and Things which Independent States may of right do. And for the support of this Declaration, with a firm reliance on the protection of divine Providence, we mutually pledge to each other our Lives, our Fortunes and our sacred Honor.

New Hampshire	Josiah Bartlett
	William Whipple
	Matthew Thornton
Massachusetts	John Hancock
	Samuel Adams
	John Adams
	Robert Treat Paine
	Elbridge Gerry
Rhode Island	Stephen Hopkins
	William Ellery
Connecticut	Roger Sherman
	Samuel Huntington
	William Williams
	Oliver Wolcott

New York	William Floyd
	Philip Livingston
	Francis Lewis
	Lewis Morris

New Jersey	Richard Stockton
	John Witherspoon
	Francis Hopkinson
	John Hart
	Abraham Clark

Pennsylvania	Robert Morris
	Benjamin Rush
	Benjamin Franklin
	John Morton
	George Clymer
	James Smith
	George Taylor
	James Wilson
	George Ross

Delaware	Caesar Rodney
	George Read
	Thomas McKean

Maryland	Samuel Chase
	William Paca
	Thomas Stone
	Charles Carroll of Carrollton

Virginia	George Wythe
	Richard Henry Lee
	Thomas Jefferson
	Benjamin Harrison
	Thomas Nelson, Jr.
	Francis Lightfoot Lee
	Carter Braxton

North Carolina	William Hooper
	Joseph Hewes
	John Penn
South Carolina	Edward Rutledge
	Thomas Heyward, Jr.
	Thomas Lynch, Jr.
	Arthur Middleton
Georgia	Button Gwinnett
	Lyman Hall
	George Walton

The Articles of Confederation

November 15, 1777

To all to whom these Presents shall come, we the undersigned Delegates of the States affixed to our Names send greeting.

Articles of Confederation and perpetual Union between the states of New Hampshire, Massachusetts-bay Rhode Island and Providence Plantations, Connecticut, New York, New Jersey, Pennsylvania, Delaware, Maryland, Virginia, North Carolina, South Carolina and Georgia.

I. The Stile of this Confederacy shall be "The United States of America".

II. Each state retains its sovereignty, freedom, and independence, and every power, jurisdiction, and right, which is not by this Confederation expressly delegated to the United States, in Congress assembled.

III. The said States hereby severally enter into a firm league of friendship with each other, for their common defense, the security of their liberties, and their mutual and general welfare, binding themselves to assist each other, against all force offered to, or attacks made upon them, or any of them, on account of religion, sovereignty, trade, or any other pretense whatever.

IV. The better to secure and perpetuate mutual friendship and intercourse among the people of the different States in this Union, the free inhabitants of each of these States, paupers, vagabonds, and fugitives from justice excepted, shall be entitled to all privileges and immunities of free citizens in the several States; and the people of each State shall free ingress and regress to and from any other State, and shall enjoy therein all the privileges of trade and commerce, subject to the same duties, impositions, and restrictions as the inhabitants thereof respectively, provided that such restrictions shall not extend so far as to prevent the removal of property imported into any State, to any other State, of which the owner is an inhabitant; provided also that no imposition, duties or restriction shall be laid by any State, on the property of the United States, or either of them.

If any person guilty of, or charged with, treason, felony, or other high misdemeanor in any State, shall flee from justice, and be found in any of the United States, he shall, upon demand of the Governor or executive power of the State from which he fled, be delivered up and removed to the State having jurisdiction of his offense.

Full faith and credit shall be given in each of these States to the records, acts, and judicial proceedings of the courts and magistrates of every other State.

V. For the most convenient management of the general interests of the United States, delegates shall be annually appointed in such manner as the legislatures of each State shall direct, to meet in Congress on the first Monday in November, in every year, with a powerreserved to each State to recall its delegates, or any of them, at any time within the year, and to send others in their stead for the remainder of the year.

No State shall be represented in Congress by less than two, nor more than seven members; and no person shall be capable of being a delegate for more than three years in any term of six years; nor shall any person, being a delegate, be capable of holding any office under the United States, for which he, or another for his benefit, receives any salary, fees or emolument of any kind.

Each State shall maintain its own delegates in a meeting of the States, and while they act as members of the committee of the States.

In determining questions in the United States in Congress assembled, each State shall have one vote.

Freedom of speech and debate in Congress shall not be impeached or questioned in any court or place out of Congress, and the members of Congress shall be protected in their persons from arrests or imprisonments, during the time of their going to and from, and attendence on Congress, except for treason, felony, or breach of the peace.

VI. No State, without the consent of the United States in Congress assembled, shall send any embassy to, or receive any embassy from, or enter into any conference, agreement, alliance or treaty with any King, Prince or State; nor shall any person holding any office of profit or trust under the United States, or any of them, accept any present, emolument, office or title of any kind whatever from any King, Prince or foreign State; nor shall the United States in Congress assembled, or any of them, grant any title of nobility.

No two or more States shall enter into any treaty, confederation or alliance whatever between them, without the consent of the United States in Congress assembled, specifying accurately the purposes for which the same is to be entered into, and how long it shall continue.

No State shall lay any imposts or duties, which may interfere with any stipulations in treaties, entered into by the United States in Congress assembled, with any King, Prince or State, in pursuance of any treaties already proposed by Congress, to the courts of France and Spain.

No vessel of war shall be kept up in time of peace by any State, except such number only, as shall be deemed necessary by the United States in Congress assembled, for the defense of such State, or its trade; nor shall any body of forces be kept up by any State in time of peace, except such number only, as in the judgement of the United States in Congress assembled, shall be deemed requisite to garrison the forts necessary for the defense of such State; but every State shall always keep up a well-regulated and disciplined militia, sufficiently armed and accoutered, and shall provide and constantly have ready for use, in public stores, a due number of filed pieces and tents, and a proper quantity of arms, ammunition and camp equipage.

No State shall engage in any war without the consent of the United States in Congress assembled, unless such State be actually invaded by enemies, or shall have received certain advice of a resolution being formed by some nation of Indians to invade such State, and the danger is so imminent as not to admit of a delay till the United States in Congress assembled can be consulted; nor shall any State grant commissions to any ships or vessels of war, nor letters of marque or reprisal, except it be after a declaration of war by the United States in Congress assembled, and then only against the Kingdom or State and the subjects thereof, against which war has been so declared, and under such regulations as shall be established by the United States in Congress assembled, unless such State be infested by pirates, in which case vessels of war may be fitted out for that occasion, and kept so long as the danger shall continue, or until the United States in Congress assembled shall determine otherwise.

VII. When land forces are raised by any State for the common defense, all officers of or under the rank of colonel, shall be appointed by the legislature of each State respectively, by whom such forces shall be raised, or in such manner as such State shall direct, and all vacancies shall be filled up by the State which first made the appointment.

VIII. All charges of war, and all other expenses that shall be incurred for the common defense or general welfare, and allowed by the United States in Congress assembled, shall be defrayed out of a common treasury, which shall be supplied by the several States in proportion to the value of all land within each State, granted or surveyed for any person, as such land and the buildings and improvements thereon shall be estimated according to such mode as the United States in Congress assembled, shall from time to time direct and appoint.

The taxes for paying that proportion shall be laid and levied by the authority and direction of the legislatures of the several States within the time agreed upon by the United

States in Congress assembled.

IX. The United States in Congress assembled, shall have the sole and exclusive right and power of determining on peace and war, except in the cases mentioned in the sixth article – of sending and receiving ambassadors – entering into treaties and alliances, provided that no treaty of commerce shall be made whereby the legislative power of the respective States shall be restrained from imposing such imposts and duties on foreigners, as their own people are subjected to, or from prohibiting the exportation or importation of any species of goods or commodities whatsoever – of establishing rules for deciding in all cases, what captures on land or water shall be legal, and in what manner prizes taken by land or naval forces in the service of the United States shall be divided or appropriated – of granting letters of marque and reprisal in times of peace – appointing courts for the trial of piracies and felonies commited on the high seas and establishing courts for receiving and determining finally appeals in all cases of captures, provided that no member of Congress shall be appointed a judge of any of the said courts.

The United States in Congress assembled shall also be the last resort on appeal in all disputes and differences now subsisting or that hereafter may arise between two or more States concerning boundary, jurisdiction or any other causes whatever; which authority shall always be exercised in the manner following. Whenever the legislative or executive authority or lawful agent of any State in controversy with another shall present a petition to Congress stating the matter in question

and praying for a hearing, notice thereof shall be given by
order of Congress to the legislative or executive authority
of the other State in controversy, and a day assigned for the
appearance of the parties by their lawful agents, who shall
then be directed to appoint by joint consent, commissioners
or judges to constitute a court for hearing and determining
the matter in question: but if they cannot agree, Congress
shall name three persons out of each of the United States, and
from the list of such persons each party shall alternately strike
out one, the petitioners beginning, until the number shall be
reduced to thirteen; and from that number not less than seven,
nor more than nine names as Congress shall direct, shall in
the presence of Congress be drawn out by lot, and the persons
whose names shall be so drawn or any five of them, shall be
commissioners or judges, to hear and finally determine the
controversy, so always as a major part of the judges who shall
hear the cause shall agree in the determination: and if either
party shall neglect to attend at the day appointed, without
showing reasons, which Congress shall judge sufficient,
or being present shall refuse to strike, the Congress shall
proceed to nominate three persons out of each State, and
the secretary of Congress shall strike in behalf of such party
absent or refusing; and the judgement and sentence of the
court to be appointed, in the manner before prescribed, shall
be final and conclusive; and if any of the parties shall refuse
to submit to the authority of such court, or to appear or defend
their claim or cause, the court shall nevertheless proceed to
pronounce sentence, or judgement, which shall in like manner
be final and decisive, the judgement or sentence and other

proceedings being in either case transmitted to Congress, and lodged among the acts of Congress for the security of the parties concerned: provided that every commissioner, before he sits in judgement, shall take an oath to be administered by one of the judges of the supreme or superior court of the State, where the cause shall be tried, 'well and truly to hear and determine the matter in question, according to the best of his judgement, without favor, affection or hope of reward': provided also, that no State shall be deprived of territory for the benefit of the United States.

All controversies concerning the private right of soil claimed under different grants of two or more States, whose jurisdictions as they may respect such lands, and the States which passed such grants are adjusted, the said grants or either of them being at the same time claimed to have originated antecedent to such settlement of jurisdiction, shall on the petition of either party to the Congress of the United States, be finally determined as near as may be in the same manner as is before prescribed for deciding disputes respecting territorial jurisdiction between different States.

The United States in Congress assembled shall also have the sole and exclusive right and power of regulating the alloy and value of coin struck by their own authority, or by that of the respective States – fixing the standards of weights and measures throughout the United States – regulating the trade and managing all affairs with the Indians, not members of any of the States, provided that the legislative right of any State within its own limits be not infringed or violated – establishing or regulating post offices from one State to another, throughout all the United States, and exacting such postage on the papers passing through the same as may be requisite to defray the expenses of the said office – appointing all officers of the land forces, in the service of the United States, excepting regimental officers – appointing all the officers of the naval forces, and commissioning all officers whatever in the service of the United States – making rules for the government and regulation of the said land and naval forces, and directing their operations.

The United States in Congress assembled shall have authority to appoint a committee, to sit in the recess of Congress, to be denominated 'A Committee of the States', and to consist of one delegate from each State; and to appoint such other committees and civil officers as may be necessary for managing the general affairs of the United States under their direction – to appoint one of their members to preside, provided that no person be allowed to serve in the office of president more than one year in any term of three years; to ascertain the necessary sums of money to be raised for the service of the United States, and to appropriate and apply the same for defraying the public expenses – to borrow money, or emit bills on the credit of the United States, transmitting every half-year to the respective States an account of the sums of money so borrowed or emitted – to build and equip a navy – to agree upon the number of land forces, and to make requisitions from each State for its quota, in proportion to the number of white inhabitants in such State; which requisition shall be binding, and thereupon the legislature of each State shall appoint the regimental officers, raise the men and cloath, arm and equip them in a solid-like manner, at the expense of the United States; and the officers and men so cloathed, armed and equipped shall march to the place appointed, and within the time agreed on by the United States in Congress assembled. But if the United States in Congress assembled shall, on consideration of circumstances judge proper that any State should not raise men, or should raise a smaller number of men than the quota thereof, such extra number shall be raised, officered, cloathed, armed and equipped in the same manner as the quota of each State, unless the legislature of such State shall judge that such extra number cannot be safely spread out in the same, in which case they shall raise, officer, cloath, arm and equip as many of such extra number as they judeg can be safely spared. And the officers and men so cloathed, armed, and equipped, shall march to the place appointed, and within the time agreed on by the United States in Congress assembled.

The United States in Congress assembled shall never engage in a war, nor grant letters of marque or reprisal in time of peace, nor enter into any treaties or alliances, nor coin money, nor regulate the value thereof, nor ascertain the sums and expenses necessary for the defense and welfare of the United States, or any of them, nor emit bills, nor borrow money on the credit of the United States, nor appropriate money, nor agree upon the number of vessels of war, to be built or purchased, or the number of land or sea forces to be raised, nor appoint a commander in chief of the army or

navy, unless nine States assent to the same: nor shall a question on any other point, except for adjourning from day to
day be determined, unless by the votes of the majority of the
United States in Congress assembled.

The Congress of the United States shall have power to
adjourn to any time within the year, and to any place within
the United States, so that no period of adjournment be for
a longer duration than the space of six months, and shall
publish the journal of their proceedings monthly, except
such parts thereof relating to treaties, alliances or military
operations, as in their judgement require secrecy; and the
yeas and nays of the delegates of each State on any question
shall be entered on the journal, when it is desired by any
delegates of a State, or any of them, at his or their request
shall be furnished with a transcript of the said journal,
except such parts as are above excepted, to lay before the
legislatures of the several States.

X. The Committee of the States, or any nine of them,
shall be authorized to execute, in the recess of Congress,
such of the powers of Congress as the United States in
Congress assembled, by the consent of the nine States,
shall from time to time think expedient to vest them with;
provided that no power be delegated to the said Committee,
for the exercise of which, by the Articles of Confederation,
the voice of nine States in the Congress of the United States
assembled be requisite.

XI. Canada acceding to this confederation, and adjoin-
ing in the measures of the United States, shall be admitted
into, and entitled to all the advantages of this Union; but no

other colony shall be admitted into the same, unless such admission be agreed to by nine States.

XII. All bills of credit emitted, monies borrowed, and debts contracted by, or under the authority of Congress, before the assembling of the United States, in pursuance of the present confederation, shall be deemed and considered as a charge against the United States, for payment and satisfaction whereof the said United States, and the public faith are hereby solemnly pleged.

XIII. Every State shall abide by the determination of the United States in Congress assembled, on all questions which by this confederation are submitted to them. And the Articles of this Confederation shall be inviolably observed by every State, and the Union shall be perpetual; nor shall any alteration at any time hereafter be made in any of them; unless such alteration be agreed to in a Congress of the United States, and be afterwards confirmed by the legislatures of every State.

And Whereas it hath pleased the Great Governor of the World to incline the hearts of the legislatures we respectively represent in Congress, to approve of, and to authorize us to ratify the said Articles of Confederation and perpetual Union. Know Ye that we the undersigned delegates, by virtue of the power and authority to us given for that purpose, do by these presents, in the name and in behalf of our respective constituents, fully and entirely ratify and confirm each and every of the said Articles of Confederation and perpetual Union, and all and singular the matters and things therein contained: And we do further solemnly plight and engage the faith of our respective constituents, that they shall abide by the determinations of the United States in Congress assembled, on all questions, which by the said Confederation are submitted to them. And that the Articles thereof shall be inviolably observed by the States we respectively represent, and that the Union shall be perpetual.

In Witness whereof we have hereunto set our hands in Congress. Done at Philadelphia in the State of Pennsylvania the ninth day of July in the Year of our Lord One Thousand Seven Hundred and Seventy-Eight, and in the Third Year of the independence of America.

Agreed to by Congress 15 November 1777 In force after ratification by Maryland, 1 March 1781

THE VIRGINIA PLAN[1]

May 29, 1787

1. Resolved that the Articles of Confederation ought to be so corrected & enlarged as to accomplish the objects proposed by their institution; namely, "common defence, security of liberty and general welfare."

2. Res^d therefore that the rights of suffrage in the National Legislature ought to be proportioned to the Quotas of contribution, or to the number of free inhabitants, as the one or the other rule may seem best in different cases.

3. Res^d that the National Legislature ought to consist of two branches.

4. Res^d that the members of the first branch of the National Legislature ought to be elected by the people of the several States every _____ for the term of _____ ; to be of the age of years at least, to receive liberal stipends by which they may be compensated for the devotion of their time to public service; to be ineligible to any office established by a particular State, or under the authority of the United States, except those peculiarly belonging to the functions of the first branch, during the term of service, and for the space of after its expiration; to be incapable of reelection for the space of after the expiration of their term of service, and to be subject to recall.

5. Resol^d that the members of the second branch of the

---

1. Also known as The Randolph Plan.

National Legislature ought to be elected by those of the first, out of a proper number of persons nominated by the individual Legislatures, to be of the age of _____ years at least; to hold their offices for a term sufficient to ensure their independency; to receive liberal stipends, by which they may be compensated for the devotion of their time to public service; and to be ineligible to any office established by a particular State, or under the authority of the United States, except those peculiarly belonging to the functions of the second branch, during the term of service, and for the space of _____ after the expiration thereof.

6. Resolved that each branch ought to possess the right of originating Acts; that the National Legislature ought to be impowered to enjoy the Legislative Rights vested in Congress bar the Confederation & moreover to legislate in all cases to which the separate States are incompetent, or in which the harmony of the United States may be interrupted by the exercise of individual Legislation; to negative all laws passed by the several States, contravening in the opinion of the National Legislature the articles of Union; and to call forth the force of the Union agst any member of the Union failing to fulfill its duty under the articles thereof.

7. Res[d] that a National Executive be instituted; to be chosen by the National Legislature for the term of years, to receive punctually at stated times, a fixed compensation for the services rendered, in which no increase or diminution shall be made so as to affect the Magistracy, existing at the time of increase or diminution, and to be ineligible a second time; and that besides a general authority to execute the

National laws, it ought to enjoy the Executive rights vested in Congress by the Confederation.

8. Res^d that the Executive and a convenient number of the National Judiciary, ought to compose a Council of revision with authority to examine every act of the National Legislature before it shall operate, & every act of a particular Legislature before a Negative thereon shall be final; and that the dissent of the said Council shall amount to a rejection, unless the Act of the National Legislature be again passed, or that of a particular Legislature be again negatived by of the members of each branch.

9. Res^d that a National Judiciary be established to consist of one or more supreme tribunals, and of inferior tribunals to be chosen by the National Legislature, to hold their offices during good behaviour; and to receive punctually at stated times fixed compensation for their services, in which no increase or diminution shall be made so as to affect the persons actually in office at the time of such increase or diminution. that the jurisdiction of the inferior tribunals shall be to hear & determine in the first instance, and of the supreme tribunal to hear and determine in the dernier resort, all piracies & felonies on the high seas, captures from an enemy; cases in which foreigners or citizens of other States applying to such jurisdictions may be interested, or which respect the collection of the National revenue; impeachments of any National officers, and questions which may involve the national peace and harmony.

10. Resolv^d that provision ought to be made for the admission of States lawfully arising within the limits of the United

States, whether from a voluntary junction of Government & Territory on otherwise, with the consent of a number of voices in the National legislature less than the whole.

11. Res[d] that a Republican Government & the territory of each State, except in the instance of a voluntary junction of Government & territory, ought to be guarantied by the United States to each State

12. Res[d] that provision ought to be made for the continuance of Congress and their authorities and privileges, until a given day after the reform of the articles of Union shall be adopted, and for the completion of all their engagements.

13. Res[d] that provision ought to be made for the amendment of the Articles of Union whensoever it shall seem necessary, and that the assent of the National Legislature ought not to be required thereto.

14. Res[d] that the Legislative Executive & Judiciary powers within the several States ought to be bound by oath to support the articles of Union.

15. Res[d] that the amendments which shall be offered to the Confederation, by the Convention ought at a proper time, or times, after the approbation of Congress to be submitted to an assembly or assemblies of Representatives, recommended by the several Legislatures to be expressly chosen by the people, to consider & decide thereon.

THE NEW JERSEY PLAN[2]
June 15, 1787

1. Resolved that the articles of Confederation ought to be so revised, corrected & enlarged, as to render the federal Constitution adequate to the exigencies of Government, & the preservation of the Union.

2. Resolved that in addition to the powers vested in the U. States in Congress, by the present existing articles of Confederation, they be authorized to pass acts for raising a revenue, by levying a duty or duties on all goods or merchandises of foreign growth or manufacture, imported into any part of the U. States, by Stamps on paper, vellum or parchment, and by a postage on all letters or packages passing through the general post-office, to be applied to such federal purposes as they shall deem proper & expedient; to make rules & regulations for the collection thereof; and the same from time to time, to alter & amend in such manner as they shall think proper: to pass Acts for the regulation of trade & commerce as well with foreign nations as with each other: provided that all punishments, fines, forfeitures & penalties to be incurred for contravening such acts rules and regulations shall be adjudged by the Common law Judiciaries of the State in which any offense contrary to the true intent & meaning of such Acts rules & regulations shall have been committed or perpetrated, with liberty of commencing in the first instance all suits & prosecutions for

2. Also known as the Small State Plan or Paterson Plan.

that purpose in the superior common law Judiciary in such State, subject nevertheless, for the correction of all errors, both in law & fact in rendering Judgment, to an appeal to the Judiciary of the U. States.

3. Resolved that whenever requisitions shall be necessary, instead of the rule for making requisitions mentioned in the articles of Confederation, the United States in Congs be authorized to make such requisitions in proportion to the whole number of white & other free citizens & inhabitants of every age sex and condition including those bound to servitude for a term of years & three fifths of all other persons not comprehended in the foregoing description, except Indians not paying taxes; that if such requisitions be not complied with, in the time specified therein, to direct the collection thereof in the non complying States & for that purpose to devise and pass acts directing & authorizing the same; provided that none of the powers hereby vested in the U. States in Congs shall be exercised without the consent of at least States, and in that proportion if the number of Confederated States should hereafter be increased or diminished.

4. Resolved that the U. States in Congs be authorized to elect a federal Executive to consist of persons, to continue in office for the term of years, to receive punctually at stated times a fixed compensation for their services, in which no increase or diminution shall be made so as to affect the persons composing the Executive at the time of such increase or diminution, to be paid out of the federal treasury; to be incapable of holding any other office or ap-

pointment during their time of service and for years thereafter; to be ineligible a second time, & removeable by Congs
on application by a majority of the Executives of the several
States; that the Executives besides their general authority to execute the federal acts ought to appoint all federal
officers not otherwise provided for, & to direct all military
operations; provided that none of the persons composing
the federal Executive shall on any occasion take command
of any troops, so as personally to conduct any enterprise as
General or in other capacity.

    5. Resolved that a federal Judiciary be established to
consist of a supreme Tribunal the Judges of which to be
appointed by the Executive, & to hold their offices during
good behaviour, to receive punctually at stated times a
fixed compensation for their services in which no increase
or diminution shall be made, so as to affect the persons
actually in office at the time of such increase or diminution;
that the Judiciary so established shall have authority to hear
& determine in the first instance on all impeachments of
federal officers, & by way of appeal in the dernier resort in
all cases touchung the rights of Ambassadors, in all cases of
captures from an enemy, in all cases of piracies & felonies
on the high Seas, in all cases in which foreigners may be
interested, in the construction of any treaty or treaties, or
which may arise on any of the Acts for regulation of trade,
or the collection of the federal Revenue: that none of the
Judiciary shall during the time they remain in office be
capable of receiving or holding any other office or appointment during their time of service, or for thereafter.

6. Resolved that all Acts of the U. States in Congs made by virtue & in pursuance of the powers hereby & by the articles of Confederation vested in them, and all Treaties made & ratified under the authority of the U. States shall be the supreme law of the respective States so far forth as those Acts or Treaties shall relate to the said States or their Citizens, and that the Judiciary of the several States shall be bound thereby in their decisions, any thing in the respective laws of the Individual States to the contrary notwithstanding; and that if any State, or any body of men in any State shall oppose or prevent ye carrying into execution such acts or treaties, the federal Executive shall be authorized to call forth ye power of the Confederated States, or so much thereof as may be necessary to enforce and compel an obedience to such Acts, or an observance of such Treaties.

7. Resolved that provision be made for the admission of new States into the Union.

8. Resolved the rule for naturalization ought to be the same in every State.

9. Resolved a Citizen of one State committing an offense in another State of the Union, shall be deemed guilty of the same offense as if it had been committed by a Citizen of the State in which the offense was committed.

HAMILTON'S PLAN OF UNION[3]

June 18, 1787

1. "The Supreme Legislative power of the United States of America to be vested in two different bodies of men; the one to be called the Assembly, the other the Senate who together shall form the Legislature of the United States with power to pass all laws whatsoever subject to the Negative hereafter mentioned.

2. The Assembly to consist of persons elected by the people to serve for three years.

3. The Senate to consist of persons elected to serve during good behaviour; their election to be made by electors chosen for that purpose by the people: in order to this the States to be divided into election districts. On the death, removal or resignation of any Senator his place to be filled out of the district from which he came.

4. The supreme Executive authority of the United States to be vested in a Governour to be elected to serve during good behaviour-the election to be made by Electors chosen by the people in the Election Districts aforesaid-The authorities & functions of the Executive to be as follows: to have a negative on all laws about to be passed, and the execution of all laws passed, to have the direction of war when authorized or begun; to have with the advice and approbation of the Senate the power of making all treaties;

---

3. Presented by Alexander Hamilton

to have the sole appointment of the heads or chief officers of the departments of Finance, War and Foreign Affairs; to have the nomination of all other officers (Ambassadors to foreign Nations included) subject to the approbation or rejection of the Senate; to have the power of pardoning all offences except Treason; which he shall not pardon without the approbation of the Senate.

5. On the death, resignation or removal of the Governour his authorities to be exercised by the President of the Senate till a Successor be appointed.

6. The Senate to have the sole power of declaring war, the power of advising and approving all Treaties, the power of approving or rejecting all appointments of officers except the heads or chiefs of the departments of Finance War and foreign affairs.

7. The supreme Judicial authority to be vested in Judges to hold their offices during good behaviour with adequate and permanent salaries. This Court to have original jurisdiction in all causes of capture, and an appellative jurisdiction in all causes in which the revenues of the general Government or the Citizens of foreign Nations are concerned.

8. The Legislature of the United States to have power to institute Courts in each State for the determination of all matters of general concern.

9. The Governour Senators and all officers of the United States to be liable to impeachment for mal- and corrupt conduct; and upon conviction to be removed from office, & disqualified for holding any place of trust or profit-All impeachments to be tried by a Court to consist of the Chief or

Judge of the superior Court of Law of each State, provided such Judge shall hold his place during good behavior, and have a permanent salary.

10. All laws of the particular States contrary to the Constitution or laws of the United States to be utterly void; and the better to prevent such laws being passed, the Governour or president of each State shall be appointed by the General Government and shall have a negative upon the laws about to be passed in the State of which he is Governour or President.

11. No State to have any forces land or Naval; and the Militia of all the States to be under the sole and exclusive direction of the United States, the officers of which to be appointed and commissioned by them.

On these several articles he entered into explanatory observations corresponding with the principles of his introductory reasoning.

Committee rose & the House Adjourned.

THE CONSTITUTION OF THE UNITED STATES

W E THE PEOPLE of the United States, in Order to form a more perfect Union, establish Justice, insure domestic Tranquility, provide for the common defence, promote the general Welfare, and secure the Blessings of Liberty to ourselves and our Posterity, do ordain and establish this Constitution for the United States of America.

Article. I.

Section. 1. All legislative Powers herein granted shall be vested in a Congress of the United States, which shall consist of a Senate and House of Representatives.

Section. 2. The House of Representatives shall be composed of Members chosen every second Year by the People of the several States, and the Electors in each State shall have the Qualifications requisite for Electors of the most numerous Branch of the State Legislature.

No Person shall be a Representative who shall not have attained to the Age of twenty five Years, and been seven Years a Citizen of the United States, and who shall not, when elected, be an Inhabitant of that State in which he shall be chosen.

[Representatives and direct Taxes shall be apportioned among the several States which may be included within this Union, according to their respective Numbers, which shall be determined by adding to the whole Number of free Persons, including those bound to Service for a Term of Years, and excluding Indians not taxed, three fifths of all other Persons.][4] The

4. Changed by section 2 of Amendment XIV

actual Enumeration shall be made within three Years after the first Meeting of the Congress of the United States, and within every subsequent Term of ten Years, in such Manner as they shall by Law direct. The Number of Representatives shall not exceed one for every thirty Thousand, but each State shall have at Least one Representative; and until such enumeration shall be made, the State of New Hampshire shall be entitled to chuse three, Massachusetts eight, Rhode-Island and Providence Plantations one, Connecticut five, New-York six, New Jersey four, Pennsylvania eight, Delaware one, Maryland six, Virginia ten, North Carolina five, South Carolina five, and Georgia three.

When vacancies happen in the Representation from any State, the Executive Authority thereof shall issue Writs of Election to fill such Vacancies.

The House of Representatives shall chuse their Speaker and other Officers; and shall have the sole Power of Impeachment.

Section. 3. The Senate of the United States shall be composed of two Senators from each State, [chosen by the Legislature thereof][5] for six Years; and each Senator shall have one Vote.

Immediately after they shall be assembled in Consequence of the first Election, they shall be divided as equally as may be into three Classes. The Seats of the Senators of the first Class shall be vacated at the Expiration of the second Year, of the second Class at the Expiration of the fourth Year, and of the third Class at the Expiration of the sixth Year, so that one third may be chosen every second Year; [and if Vacancies happen by Resignation, or otherwise, during the

---

5. Changed by Amendment XVII

Recess of the Legislature of any State, the Executive thereof may make temporary Appointments until the next Meeting of the Legislature, which shall then fill such Vacancies.][6]

No Person shall be a Senator who shall not have attained to the Age of thirty Years, and been nine Years a Citizen of the United States, and who shall not, when elected, be an Inhabitant of that State for which he shall be chosen.

The Vice President of the United States shall be President of the Senate, but shall have no Vote, unless they be equally divided.

The Senate shall chuse their other Officers, and also a President pro tempore, in the Absence of the Vice President, or when he shall exercise the Office of President of the United States.

The Senate shall have the sole Power to try all Impeachments. When sitting for that Purpose, they shall be on Oath or Affirmation. When the President of the United States is tried, the Chief Justice shall preside: And no Person shall be convicted without the Concurrence of two thirds of the Members present.

Judgment in Cases of Impeachment shall not extend further than to removal from Office, and disqualification to hold and enjoy any Office of honor, Trust or Profit under the United States: but the Party convicted shall nevertheless be liable and subject to Indictment, Trial, Judgment and Punishment, according to Law.

Section. 4. The Times, Places and Manner of holding Elections for Senators and Representatives, shall be prescribed in each State by the Legislature thereof; but the Con-

---

6. Changed by Amendment XVII

gress may at any time by Law make or alter such Regulations, except as to the Places of chusing Senators.

The Congress shall assemble at least once in every Year, and such Meeting shall be [on the first Monday in December,][7] unless they shall by Law appoint a different Day.

Section. 5. Each House shall be the Judge of the Elections, Returns and Qualifications of its own Members, and a Majority of each shall constitute a Quorum to do Business; but a smaller Number may adjourn from day to day, and may be authorized to compel the Attendance of absent Members, in such Manner, and under such Penalties as each House may provide.

Each House may determine the Rules of its Proceedings, punish its Members for disorderly Behaviour, and, with the Concurrence of two thirds, expel a Member.

Each House shall keep a Journal of its Proceedings, and from time to time publish the same, excepting such Parts as may in their Judgment require Secrecy; and the Yeas and Nays of the Members of either House on any question shall, at the Desire of one fifth of those Present, be entered on the Journal.

Neither House, during the Session of Congress, shall, without the Consent of the other, adjourn for more than three days, nor to any other Place than that in which the two Houses shall be sitting.

Section. 6. The Senators and Representatives shall receive a Compensation for their Services, to be ascertained by Law, and paid out of the Treasury of the United States. They shall in all Cases, except Treason, Felony and Breach of the

7. Changed by Section 2 of Amendment XX

Peace, be privileged from Arrest during their Attendance at the Session of their respective Houses, and in going to and returning from the same; and for any Speech or Debate in either House, they shall not be questioned in any other Place.

No Senator or Representative shall, during the Time for which he was elected, be appointed to any civil Office under the Authority of the United States, which shall have been created, or the Emoluments whereof shall have been en-creased during such time; and no Person holding any Office under the United States, shall be a Member of either House during his Continuance in Office.

Section. 7. All Bills for raising Revenue shall originate in the House of Representatives; but the Senate may propose or concur with Amendments as on other Bills.

Every Bill which shall have passed the House of Representatives and the Senate, shall, before it become a Law, be presented to the President of the United States: If he approve he shall sign it, but if not he shall return it, with his Objections to that House in which it shall have originated, who shall enter the Objections at large on their Journal, and proceed to reconsider it. If after such Reconsideration two thirds of that House shall agree to pass the Bill, it shall be sent, together with the Objections, to the other House, by which it shall likewise be reconsidered, and if approved by two thirds of that House, it shall become a Law. But in all such Cases the Votes of both Houses shall be determined by yeas and Nays, and the Names of the Persons voting for and against the Bill shall be entered on the Journal of each House respectively. If any Bill shall not be returned by the President within ten Days (Sundays excepted) after it shall have been presented to him, the Same shall be a Law, in like Manner as if he had signed it, unless the Congress by their Adjournment prevent its Return, in which Case it shall not be a Law.

Every Order, Resolution, or Vote to which the Concurrence of the Senate and House of Representatives may be necessary (except on a question of Adjournment) shall be presented to the President of the United States; and before the Same shall take Effect, shall be approved by him, or being disapproved by him, shall be repassed by two thirds of the Senate and House of Representatives, according to the Rules and Limitations prescribed in the Case of a Bill.

Section. 8. The Congress shall have Power To lay and collect Taxes, Duties, Imposts and Excises, to pay the Debts and provide for the common Defence and general Welfare of the United States; but all Duties, Imposts and Excises shall be uniform throughout the United States;

To borrow Money on the credit of the United States;

To regulate Commerce with foreign Nations, and among the several States, and with the Indian Tribes;

To establish an uniform Rule of Naturalization, and uniform Laws on the subject of Bankruptcies throughout the United States;

To coin Money, regulate the Value thereof, and of foreign Coin, and fix the Standard of Weights and Measures;

To provide for the Punishment of counterfeiting the Securities and current Coin of the United States;

To establish Post Offices and post Roads;

To promote the Progress of Science and useful Arts, by

securing for limited Times to Authors and Inventors the exclusive Right to their respective Writings and Discoveries;

To constitute Tribunals inferior to the supreme Court;

To define and punish Piracies and Felonies committed on the high Seas, and Offences against the Law of Nations;

To declare War, grant Letters of Marque and Reprisal, and make Rules concerning Captures on Land and Water;

To raise and support Armies, but no Appropriation of Money to that Use shall be for a longer Term than two Years;

To provide and maintain a Navy;

To make Rules for the Government and Regulation of the land and naval Forces;

To provide for calling forth the Militia to execute the Laws of the Union, suppress Insurrections and repel Invasions;

To provide for organizing, arming, and disciplining, the Militia, and for governing such Part of them as may be employed in the Service of the United States, reserving to the States respectively, the Appointment of the Officers, and the Authority of training the Militia according to the discipline prescribed by Congress;

To exercise exclusive Legislation in all Cases whatsoever, over such District (not exceeding ten Miles square) as may, by Cession of particular States, and the Acceptance of Congress, become the Seat of the Government of the United States, and to exercise like Authority over all Places purchased by the Consent of the Legislature of the State in which the Same shall be, for the Erection of Forts, Magazines, Arsenals, dock-Yards, and other needful Buildings;–And

To make all Laws which shall be necessary and proper for carrying into Execution the foregoing Powers, and all other Powers vested by this Constitution in the Government of the United States, or in any Department or Officer thereof.

Section. 9. The Migration or Importation of such Persons as any of the States now existing shall think proper to admit, shall not be prohibited by the Congress prior to the Year one thousand eight hundred and eight, but a Tax or duty may be imposed on such Importation, not exceeding ten dollars for each Person.

The Privilege of the Writ of Habeas Corpus shall not be suspended, unless when in Cases of Rebellion or Invasion the public Safety may require it.

No Bill of Attainder or ex post facto Law shall be passed.

No Capitation, or other direct, Tax shall be laid, [unless in Proportion to the Census or enumeration herein before directed to be taken.][8]

No Tax or Duty shall be laid on Articles exported from any State.

No Preference shall be given by any Regulation of Commerce or Revenue to the Ports of one State over those of another; nor shall Vessels bound to, or from, one State, be obliged to enter, clear, or pay Duties in another.

No Money shall be drawn from the Treasury, but in Consequence of Appropriations made by Law; and a regular Statement and Account of the Receipts and Expenditures of all public Money shall be published from time to time.

No Title of Nobility shall be granted by the United States:

---

8. See Amendment XVI

And no Person holding any Office of Profit or Trust under them, shall, without the Consent of the Congress, accept of any present, Emolument, Office, or Title, of any kind whatever, from any King, Prince, or foreign State.

Section. 10. No State shall enter into any Treaty, Alliance, or Confederation; grant Letters of Marque and Reprisal; coin Money; emit Bills of Credit; make any Thing but gold and silver Coin a Tender in Payment of Debts; pass any Bill of Attainder, ex post facto Law, or Law impairing the Obligation of Contracts, or grant any Title of Nobility.

No State shall, without the Consent of the Congress, lay any Imposts or Duties on Imports or Exports, except what may be absolutely necessary for executing it's inspection Laws: and the net Produce of all Duties and Imposts, laid by any State on Imports or Exports, shall be for the Use of the Treasury of the United States; and all such Laws shall be subject to the Revision and Controul of the Congress.

No State shall, without the Consent of Congress, lay any Duty of Tonnage, keep Troops, or Ships of War in time of Peace, enter into any Agreement or Compact with another State, or with a foreign Power, or engage in War, unless actually invaded, or in such imminent Danger as will not admit of delay.

Article. II.

Section. 1. The executive Power shall be vested in a President of the United States of America. He shall hold his Office during the Term of four Years, and, together with the Vice President, chosen for the same Term, be elected, as follows:

Each State shall appoint, in such Manner as the Legislature thereof may direct, a Number of Electors, equal to the whole Number of Senators and Representatives to which the State may be entitled in the Congress: but no Senator or Representative, or Person holding an Office of Trust or Profit under the United States, shall be appointed an Elector.

[The Electors shall meet in their respective States, and vote by Ballot for two Persons, of whom one at least shall not be an Inhabitant of the same State with themselves. And they shall make a List of all the Persons voted for, and of the Number of Votes for each; which List they shall sign and certify, and transmit sealed to the Seat of the Government of the United States, directed to the President of the Senate. The President of the Senate shall, in the Presence of the Senate and House of Representatives, open all the Certificates, and the Votes shall then be counted. The Person having the greatest Number of Votes shall be the President, if such Number be a Majority of the whole Number of Electors appointed; and if there be more than one who have such Majority, and have an equal Number of Votes, then the House of Representatives shall immediately chuse by Ballot one of them for President; and if no Person have a Majority, then from the five highest on the List the said House shall in like Manner chuse the President. But in chusing the President, the Votes shall be taken by States, the Representation from each State having one Vote; A quorum for this purpose shall consist of a Member or Members from two thirds of the States, and a Majority of all the States shall be necessary to a Choice. In every Case, after the Choice of the President, the Person having the greatest Number of Votes of the Electors shall be the Vice President. But if there should remain two or more who have equal Votes, the Senate shall chuse from them by Ballot the Vice President.]⁹

The Congress may determine the Time of chusing the Electors, and the Day on which they shall give their Votes; which Day shall be the same throughout the United States.

No Person except a natural born Citizen, or a Citizen of the United States, at the time of the Adoption of this Constitution, shall be eligible to the Office of President; neither shall any Person be eligible to that Office who shall not have attained to the Age of thirty five Years, and been fourteen Years a Resident within the United States.

[In Case of the Removal of the President from Office, or of his Death, Resignation, or Inability to discharge the Powers and Duties of the said Office, the Same shall devolve on the Vice President, and the Congress may by Law provide for the Case of Removal, Death, Resignation or Inability, both of the President and Vice President, declaring what Officer shall then act as President, and such Officer shall act accordingly, until the Disability be removed, or a President shall be elected.]¹⁰

The President shall, at stated Times, receive for his Services, a Compensation, which shall neither be increased nor diminished during the Period for which he shall have been elected, and he shall not receive within that Period any other Emolument from the United States, or any of them.

Before he enter on the Execution of his Office, he shall take the following Oath or Affirmation:– "I do solemnly swear (or affirm) that I will faithfully execute the Office of President of

9. Changed by Amendment XII

10. Changed by Amendment XXV

the United States, and will to the best of my Ability, preserve, protect and defend the Constitution of the United States."

Section. 2. The President shall be Commander in Chief of the Army and Navy of the United States, and of the Militia of the several States, when called into the actual Service of the United States; he may require the Opinion, in writing, of the principal Officer in each of the executive Departments, upon any Subject relating to the Duties of their respective Offices, and he shall have Power to grant Reprieves and Pardons for Offences against the United States, except in Cases of Impeachment.

He shall have Power, by and with the Advice and Consent of the Senate, to make Treaties, provided two thirds of the Senators present concur; and he shall nominate, and by and with the Advice and Consent of the Senate, shall appoint Ambassadors, other public Ministers and Consuls, Judges of the supreme Court, and all other Officers of the United States, whose Appointments are not herein otherwise provided for, and which shall be established by Law: but the Congress may by Law vest the Appointment of such inferior Officers, as they think proper, in the President alone, in the Courts of Law, or in the Heads of Departments.

The President shall have Power to fill up all Vacancies that may happen during the Recess of the Senate, by granting Commissions which shall expire at the End of their next Session.

Section. 3. He shall from time to time give to the Congress Information of the State of the Union, and recommend to their Consideration such Measures as he shall judge necessary and expedient; he may, on extraordinary Occasions, convene both Houses, or either of them, and in Case of Disagreement between them, with Respect to the Time of Adjournment, he may adjourn them to such Time as he shall think proper; he shall receive Ambassadors and other public Ministers; he shall take Care that the Laws be faithfully executed, and shall Commission all the Officers of the United States.

Section. 4. The President, Vice President and all civil Officers of the United States, shall be removed from Office on Impeachment for, and Conviction of, Treason, Bribery, or other high Crimes and Misdemeanors.

Article III.

Section. 1. The judicial Power of the United States shall be vested in one supreme Court, and in such inferior Courts as the Congress may from time to time ordain and establish. The Judges, both of the supreme and inferior Courts, shall hold their Offices during good Behaviour, and shall, at stated Times, receive for their Services a Compensation, which shall not be diminished during their Continuance in Office.

Section. 2. The judicial Power shall extend to all Cases, in Law and Equity, arising under this Constitution, the Laws of the United States, and Treaties made, or which shall be made, under their Authority;–to all Cases affecting Ambassadors, other public Ministers and Consuls;–to all Cases of admiralty and maritime Jurisdiction;–to Controversies to which the United States shall be a Party;–to Controversies between two or more States;– [between a State and Citizens of another State;–][11] between Citizens of different States;– between Citizens of the same State claiming Lands under Grants of different States, [and between a State, or the Citizens thereof, and foreign States, Citizens or Subjects.][12]

In all Cases affecting Ambassadors, other public Ministers and Consuls, and those in which a State shall be Party, the supreme Court shall have original Jurisdiction. In all the other Cases before mentioned, the supreme Court shall have appellate Jurisdiction, both as to Law and Fact, with such Exceptions, and under such Regulations as the Congress shall make.

The Trial of all Crimes, except in Cases of Impeachment, shall be by Jury; and such Trial shall be held in the State where the said Crimes shall have been committed; but when not committed within any State, the Trial shall be at such Place or Places as the Congress may by Law have directed.

Section. 3. Treason against the United States, shall consist only in levying War against them, or in adhering to their Enemies, giving them Aid and Comfort. No Person shall be convicted of Treason unless on the Testimony of two Witnesses to the same overt Act, or on Confession in open Court.

The Congress shall have Power to declare the Punishment of Treason, but no Attainder of Treason shall work Corruption of Blood, or Forfeiture except during the Life of the Person attainted.

Article. IV.

Section. 1. Full Faith and Credit shall be given in each State to the public Acts, Records, and judicial Proceedings

11. Changed by Amendment XI
12. Changed by Amendment XI

of every other State. And the Congress may by general Laws prescribe the Manner in which such Acts, Records and Proceedings shall be proved, and the Effect thereof.

Section. 2. The Citizens of each State shall be entitled to all Privileges and Immunities of Citizens in the several States.

A Person charged in any State with Treason, Felony, or other Crime, who shall flee from Justice, and be found in another State, shall on Demand of the executive Authority of the State from which he fled, be delivered up, to be removed to the State having Jurisdiction of the Crime.

[No Person held to Service or Labour in one State, under the Laws thereof, escaping into another, shall, in Consequence of any Law or Regulation therein, be discharged from such Service or Labour, but shall be delivered up on Claim of the Party to whom such Service or Labour may be due.][13]

Section. 3. New States may be admitted by the Congress into this Union; but no new State shall be formed or erected within the Jurisdiction of any other State; nor any State be formed by the Junction of two or more States, or Parts of States, without the Consent of the Legislatures of the States concerned as well as of the Congress.

The Congress shall have Power to dispose of and make all needful Rules and Regulations respecting the Territory or other Property belonging to the United States; and nothing in this Constitution shall be so construed as to Prejudice any Claims of the United States, or of any particular State.

Section. 4. The United States shall guarantee to every State in this Union a Republican Form of Government, and

---

13. Changed by Amendment XIII

shall protect each of them against Invasion; and on Application of the Legislature, or of the Executive (when the Legislature cannot be convened), against domestic Violence.

Article. V.

The Congress, whenever two thirds of both Houses shall deem it necessary, shall propose Amendments to this Constitution, or, on the Application of the Legislatures of two thirds of the several States, shall call a Convention for proposing Amendments, which, in either Case, shall be valid to all Intents and Purposes, as Part of this Constitution, when ratified by the Legislatures of three fourths of the several States, or by Conventions in three fourths thereof, as the one or the other Mode of Ratification may be proposed by the Congress; Provided that no Amendment which may be made prior to the Year One thousand eight hundred and eight shall in any Manner affect the first and fourth Clauses in the Ninth Section of the first Article; and that no State, without its Consent, shall be deprived of its equal Suffrage in the Senate.

Article. VI.

All Debts contracted and Engagements entered into, before the Adoption of this Constitution, shall be as valid against the United States under this Constitution, as under the Confederation.

This Constitution, and the Laws of the United States which shall be made in Pursuance thereof; and all Treaties made, or which shall be made, under the Authority of the United States, shall be the supreme Law of the Land; and the Judges in every State shall be bound thereby, any Thing in the Constitution or

Laws of any State to the Contrary notwithstanding.

The Senators and Representatives before mentioned, and the Members of the several State Legislatures, and all executive and judicial Officers, both of the United States and of the several States, shall be bound by Oath or Affirmation, to support this Constitution; but no religious Test shall ever be required as a Qualification to any Office or public Trust under the United States.

Article. VII.

The Ratification of the Conventions of nine States, shall be sufficient for the Establishment of this Constitution between the States so ratifying the Same.

The Word, "the," being interlined between the seventh and eighth Lines of the first Page, the Word "Thirty" being partly written on an Erazure in the fifteenth Line of the first Page, The Words "is tried" being interlined between the thirty second and thirty third Lines of the first Page and the Word "the" being interlined between the forty third and forty fourth Lines of the second Page.

Done in Convention by the Unanimous Consent of the States present the Seventeenth Day of September in the Year of our Lord one thousand seven hundred and Eighty seven and of the Independence of the United States of America the Twelfth In witness whereof We have hereunto subscribed our Names,

G°. Washington
Presidt and deputy from Virginia

Delaware	Geo: Read
	Gunning Bedford jun
	John Dickinson
	Richard Bassett
	Jaco: Broom
Maryland	James McHenry
	Dan of St Thos. Jenifer
	Danl. Carroll
Virginia	John Blair
	James Madison Jr.
North Carolina	Wm. Blount
	Richd. Dobbs Spaight
	Hu Williamson
South Carolina	J. Rutledge
	Charles Cotesworth Pinckney
	Charles Pinckney
	Pierce Butler
Georgia	William Few
	Abr Baldwin
New Hampshire	John Langdon
	Nicholas Gilman
Massachusetts	Nathaniel Gorham
	Rufus King
Connecticut	Wm. Saml. Johnson
	Roger Sherman
New York	Alexander Hamilton

New Jersey	Wil: Livingston
	David Brearley
	Wm. Paterson
	Jona: Dayton
Pennsylvania	B Franklin
	Thomas Mifflin
	Robt. Morris
	Geo. Clymer
	Thos. FitzSimons
	Jared Ingersoll
	James Wilson
	Gouv Morris

Attest William Jackson Secretary

AMENDMENTS
TO THE CONSTITUTION

The Preamble to The Bill of Rights[14]

Congress of the United States begun and held at the City of New-York, on Wednesday the fourth of March, one thousand seven hundred and eighty nine.

THE Conventions of a number of the States, having at the time of their adopting the Constitution, expressed a desire, in order to prevent misconstruction or abuse of its powers, that further declaratory and restrictive clauses should be added: And as extending the ground of public confidence in the Government, will best ensure the beneficent ends of its institution.

RESOLVED by the Senate and House of Representatives of the United States of America, in Congress assembled, two thirds of both Houses concurring, that the following Articles be proposed to the Legislatures of the several States, as amendments to the Constitution of the United States, all, or any of which Articles, when ratified by three fourths of the said Legislatures, to be valid to all intents and purposes, as part of the said Constitution; viz.

ARTICLES in addition to, and Amendment of the Constitution of the United States of America, proposed by Congress, and ratified by the Legislatures of the several States, pursuant to the fifth Article of the original Constitution.

---

14. The Bill of Rights (Amendments I - X) was ratified December 15, 1791.

Amendment I

Congress shall make no law respecting an establishment of religion, or prohibiting the free exercise thereof; or abridging the freedom of speech, or of the press; or the right of the people peaceably to assemble, and to petition the Government for a redress of grievances.

Amendment II

A well regulated Militia being necessary to the security of a free State, the right of the people to keep and bear Arms shall not be infringed.

Amendment III

No Soldier shall, in time of peace be quartered in any house, without the consent of the Owner, nor in time of war, but in a manner to be prescribed by law.

Amendment IV

The right of the people to be secure in their persons, houses, papers, and effects, against unreasonable searches and seizures, shall not be violated, and no Warrants shall issue, but upon probable cause, supported by Oath or affirmation, and particularly describing the place to be searched, and the persons or things to be seized.

Amendment V

No person shall be held to answer for a capital, or otherwise infamous crime, unless on a presentment or indictment of a Grand Jury, except in cases arising in the land or naval forces, or in the Militia, when in actual service in time of War or public danger; nor shall any person be subject for the same offence to be twice put in jeopardy of life or limb; nor shall be compelled in any criminal case to be a witness against himself, nor be deprived of life, liberty, or property, without due process of law; nor shall private property be taken for public use, without just compensation.

Amendment VI

In all criminal prosecutions, the accused shall enjoy the right to a speedy and public trial, by an impartial jury of the State and district wherein the crime shall have been committed, which district shall have been previously ascertained by law, and to be informed of the nature and cause of the accusation; to be confronted with the witnesses against him; to have compulsory process for obtaining witnesses in his favor, and to have the Assistance of Counsel for his defence.

Amendment VII

In suits at common law, where the value in controversy shall exceed twenty dollars, the right of trial by jury shall be preserved, and no fact tried by a jury, shall be otherwise reexamined in any Court of the United States, than according to the rules of the common law.

Amendment VIII

Excessive bail shall not be required, nor excessive fines imposed, nor cruel and unusual punishments inflicted.

Amendment IX

The enumeration in the Constitution, of certain rights, shall not be construed to deny or disparage others retained by the people.

Amendment X

The powers not delegated to the United States by the Constitution, nor prohibited by it to the States, are reserved to the States respectively, or to the people.

Amendment XI[15]

The Judicial power of the United States shall not be construed to extend to any suit in law or equity, commenced or prosecuted against one of the United States by Citizens of another State, or by Citizens or Subjects of any Foreign State.

Amendment XII[16]

The Electors shall meet in their respective states and vote by ballot for President and Vice-President, one of whom, at least, shall not be an inhabitant of the same state with themselves; they shall name in their ballots the person voted for as President, and in distinct ballots the person voted for as Vice-President, and they shall make distinct lists of all persons voted for as President, and of all persons voted for as Vice-President, and of the number of votes for each, which lists they shall sign and certify, and transmit sealed to the seat of the government of the United States, directed to the President of the Senate; — the President of the Senate shall, in the presence of the Senate and House of Representatives, open all the certificates and the votes shall then be counted; — The person having the greatest number of votes for President, shall be the President, if such number be a majority of the whole number of Electors appointed; and if no person have such majority, then from the persons

15. Ratified February 7, 1795
16. Ratified June 15, 1804

having the highest numbers not exceeding three on the list of those voted for as President, the House of Representatives shall choose immediately, by ballot, the President. But in choosing the President, the votes shall be taken by states, the representation from each state having one vote; a quorum for this purpose shall consist of a member or members from two-thirds of the states, and a majority of all the states shall be necessary to a choice. [And if the House of Representatives shall not choose a President whenever the right of choice shall devolve upon them, before the fourth day of March next following, then the Vice-President shall act as President, as in case of the death or other constitutional disability of the President. —][17] The person having the greatest number of votes as Vice-President, shall be the Vice-President, if such number be a majority of the whole number of Electors appointed, and if no person have a majority, then from the two highest numbers on the list, the Senate shall choose the Vice-President; a quorum for the purpose shall consist of two-thirds of the whole number of Senators, and a majority of the whole number shall be necessary to a choice. But no person constitutionally ineligible to the office of President shall be eligible to that of Vice-President of the United States.

Amendment XIII[18]

Section 1. Neither slavery nor involuntary servitude, except as a punishment for crime whereof the party shall have been duly convicted, shall exist within the United States, or any place subject to their jurisdiction.

17. Superseded by section 3 of Amendment XX
18. Ratified December 6, 1865

Section 2. Congress shall have power to enforce this article by appropriate legislation.

Amendment XIV[19]

Section 1. All persons born or naturalized in the United States, and subject to the jurisdiction thereof, are citizens of the United States and of the State wherein they reside. No State shall make or enforce any law which shall abridge the privileges or immunities of citizens of the United States; nor shall any State deprive any person of life, liberty, or property, without due process of law; nor deny to any person within its jurisdiction the equal protection of the laws.

Section 2. Representatives shall be apportioned among the several States according to their respective numbers, counting the whole number of persons in each State, excluding Indians not taxed. But when the right to vote at any election for the choice of electors for President and Vice-President of the United States, Representatives in Congress, the Executive and Judicial officers of a State, or the members of the Legislature thereof, is denied to any of the male inhabitants of such State, being twenty-one years of age, and citizens of the United States, or in any way abridged, except for participation in rebellion, or other crime, the basis of representation therein shall be reduced in the proportion which the number of such male citizens shall bear to the whole number of male citizens twenty-one years of age in such State.

Section 3. No person shall be a Senator or Representative in Congress, or elector of President and Vice-President,

---

19. Ratified July 9, 1868

or hold any office, civil or military, under the United States, or under any State, who, having previously taken an oath, as a member of Congress, or as an officer of the United States, or as a member of any State legislature, or as an executive or judicial officer of any State, to support the Constitution of the United States, shall have engaged in insurrection or rebellion against the same, or given aid or comfort to the enemies thereof. But Congress may by a vote of two-thirds of each House, remove such disability.

Section 4. The validity of the public debt of the United States, authorized by law, including debts incurred for payment of pensions and bounties for services in suppressing insurrection or rebellion, shall not be questioned. But neither the United States nor any State shall assume or pay any debt or obligation incurred in aid of insurrection or rebellion against the United States, or any claim for the loss or emancipation of any slave; but all such debts, obligations and claims shall be held illegal and void.

Section 5. The Congress shall have the power to enforce, by appropriate legislation, the provisions of this article.

Amendment XV[20]

Section 1. The right of citizens of the United States to vote shall not be denied or abridged by the United States or by any State on account of race, color, or previous condition of servitude—

Section 2. The Congress shall have the power to enforce this article by appropriate legislation.

---

20. Ratified February 3, 1870

Amendment XVI[21]

The Congress shall have power to lay and collect taxes on incomes, from whatever source derived, without apportionment among the several States, and without regard to any census or enumeration.

Amendment XVII[22]

The Senate of the United States shall be composed of two Senators from each State, elected by the people thereof, for six years; and each Senator shall have one vote. The electors in each State shall have the qualifications requisite for electors of the most numerous branch of the State legislatures.

When vacancies happen in the representation of any State in the Senate, the executive authority of such State shall issue writs of election to fill such vacancies: Provided, That the legislature of any State may empower the executive thereof to make temporary appointments until the people fill the vacancies by election as the legislature may direct.

This amendment shall not be so construed as to affect the election or term of any Senator chosen before it becomes valid as part of the Constitution.

Amendment XVIII[23]

[**Section 1.** After one year from the ratification of this article the manufacture, sale, or transportation of intoxicating

---

21. Ratified February 3, 1913

22. Ratified April 8, 1913

23. Amendment XVIII was ratified January 16, 1919. It was repealed by Amendment XXI, December 5, 1933.

liquors within, the importation thereof into, or the exportation thereof from the United States and all territory subject to the jurisdiction thereof for beverage purposes is hereby prohibited.

Section 2. The Congress and the several States shall have concurrent power to enforce this article by appropriate legislation.

Section 3. This article shall be inoperative unless it shall have been ratified as an amendment to the Constitution by the legislatures of the several States, as provided in the Constitution, within seven years from the date of the submission hereof to the States by the Congress.]

Amendment XIX[24]

The right of citizens of the United States to vote shall not be denied or abridged by the United States or by any State on account of sex.

Congress shall have power to enforce this article by appropriate legislation.

Amendment XX[25]

Section 1. The terms of the President and the Vice President shall end at noon on the 20th day of January, and the terms of Senators and Representatives at noon on the 3d day of January, of the years in which such terms would have ended if this article had not been ratified; and the terms of their successors shall then begin.

Section 2. The Congress shall assemble at least once in

24. Ratified August 18, 1920
25. Ratified January 23, 1933

every year, and such meeting shall begin at noon on the 3d day of January, unless they shall by law appoint a different day.

Section 3. If, at the time fixed for the beginning of the term of the President, the President elect shall have died, the Vice President elect shall become President. If a President shall not have been chosen before the time fixed for the beginning of his term, or if the President elect shall have failed to qualify, then the Vice President elect shall act as President until a President shall have qualified; and the Congress may by law provide for the case wherein neither a President elect nor a Vice President shall have qualified, declaring who shall then act as President, or the manner in which one who is to act shall be selected, and such person shall act accordingly until a President or Vice President shall have qualified.

Section 4. The Congress may by law provide for the case of the death of any of the persons from whom the House of Representatives may choose a President whenever the right of choice shall have devolved upon them, and for the case of the death of any of the persons from whom the Senate may choose a Vice President whenever the right of choice shall have devolved upon them.

Section 5. Sections 1 and 2 shall take effect on the 15th day of October following the ratification of this article.

Section 6. This article shall be inoperative unless it shall have been ratified as an amendment to the Constitution by the legislatures of three-fourths of the several States within seven years from the date of its submission.

Amendment XXI[26]

Section 1. The eighteenth article of amendment to the Constitution of the United States is hereby repealed.

Section 2. The transportation or importation into any State, Territory, or Possession of the United States for delivery or use therein of intoxicating liquors, in violation of the laws thereof, is hereby prohibited.

Section 3. This article shall be inoperative unless it shall have been ratified as an amendment to the Constitution by conventions in the several States, as provided in the Constitution, within seven years from the date of the submission hereof to the States by the Congress.

Amendment XXII[27]

Section 1. No person shall be elected to the office of the President more than twice, and no person who has held the office of President, or acted as President, for more than two years of a term to which some other person was elected President shall be elected to the office of President more than once. But this Article shall not apply to any person holding the office of President when this Article was proposed by Congress, and shall not prevent any person who may be holding the office of President, or acting as President, during the term within which this Article becomes operative from holding the office of President or acting as President during the remainder of such term.

Section 2. This article shall be inoperative unless it shall have been ratified as an amendment to the Constitution by the legis-

---

26. Ratified December 5, 1933
27. Ratified February 27, 1951

latures of three-fourths of the several States within seven years from the date of its submission to the States by the Congress.

Amendment XXIII[28]

Section 1. The District constituting the seat of Government of the United States shall appoint in such manner as Congress may direct:

A number of electors of President and Vice President equal to the whole number of Senators and Representatives in Congress to which the District would be entitled if it were a State, but in no event more than the least populous State; they shall be in addition to those appointed by the States, but they shall be considered, for the purposes of the election of President and Vice President, to be electors appointed by a State; and they shall meet in the District and perform such duties as provided by the twelfth article of amendment.

Section 2. The Congress shall have power to enforce this article by appropriate legislation.

Amendment XXIV[29]

Section 1. The right of citizens of the United States to vote in any primary or other election for President or Vice President, for electors for President or Vice President, or for Senator or Representative in Congress, shall not be denied or abridged by the United States or any State by reason of failure to pay poll tax or other tax.

Section 2. The Congress shall have power to enforce this article by appropriate legislation.

---

28. Ratified March 29, 1961
29. Ratified January 23, 1964

Amendment XXV[30]

Section 1. In case of the removal of the President from office or of his death or resignation, the Vice President shall become President.

Section 2. Whenever there is a vacancy in the office of the Vice President, the President shall nominate a Vice President who shall take office upon confirmation by a majority vote of both Houses of Congress.

Section 3. Whenever the President transmits to the President pro tempore of the Senate and the Speaker of the House of Representatives his written declaration that he is unable to discharge the powers and duties of his office, and until he transmits to them a written declaration to the contrary, such powers and duties shall be discharged by the Vice President as Acting President.

Section 4. Whenever the Vice President and a majority of either the principal officers of the executive departments or of such other body as Congress may by law provide, transmit to the President pro tempore of the Senate and the Speaker of the House of Representatives their written declaration that the President is unable to discharge the powers and duties of his office, the Vice President shall immediately assume the powers and duties of the office as Acting President.

Thereafter, when the President transmits to the President pro tempore of the Senate and the Speaker of the House of Representatives his written declaration that no inability exists, he shall resume the powers and duties of his office unless the Vice President and a majority of either the principal officers of the

30. Ratified February 10, 1967

executive department or of such other body as Congress may by law provide, transmit within four days to the President pro tempore of the Senate and the Speaker of the House of Representatives their written declaration that the President is unable to discharge the powers and duties of his office. Thereupon Congress shall decide the issue, assembling within forty-eight hours for that purpose if not in session. If the Congress, within twenty-one days after receipt of the latter written declaration, or, if Congress is not in session, within twenty-one days after Congress is required to assemble, determines by two-thirds vote of both Houses that the President is unable to discharge the powers and duties of his office, the Vice President shall continue to discharge the same as Acting President; otherwise, the President shall resume the powers and duties of his office.

Amendment XXVI[31]

Section 1. The right of citizens of the United States, who are eighteen years of age or older, to vote shall not be denied or abridged by the United States or by any State on account of age.

Section 2. The Congress shall have power to enforce this article by appropriate legislation.

Amendment XXVII[32]

No law, varying the compensation for the services of the Senators and Representatives, shall take effect, until an election of representatives shall have intervened.

---

31. Ratified July 1, 1971
32. Ratified May 7, 1992

ESSENTIAL LIBERTY
IN THE WORDS OF
OUR FOUNDERS

Declaration of Independence:
"Endowed by their Creator"

[I]t is a common observation here that our cause is the
cause of all mankind, and that we are fighting for their
liberty in defending our own. ... We must all hang together,
or assuredly we shall all hang separately.
– *Benjamin Franklin* –

It ought to be commemorated, as the Day of Deliverance
by solemn Acts of Devotion to God Almighty. It ought to
be solemnized with Pomp and Parade, with Shows, Games,
Sports, guns, Bells, Bonfires and Illuminations from one
End of this Continent to the other from this Time forward
forever more. You will think me transported with Enthusi-
asm but I am not. I am well aware of the Toil and Blood and
Treasure, that it will cost Us to maintain this Declaration,
and support and defend these States. Yet through all the
Gloom I can see the Rays of ravishing Light and Glory. I
can see that the End is more than worth all the Means. And
that Posterity will tryumph in that Days Transaction, even
altho We should rue it, which I trust in God We shall not.
– *John Adams* –

There! His Majesty can now read my name without glasses. And he can double the reward on my head!
– *John Hancock* –

The Declaration of Independence... [is the] declaratory charter of our rights, and the rights of man. ... [T]he flames kindled on the 4 of July 1776, have spread over too much of the globe to be extinguished by the feeble engines of despotism; on the contrary, they will consume these engines and all who work them. ... This was the object of the Declaration of Independence. Not to find out new principles, or new arguments, never before thought of, not merely to say things which had never been said before; but to place before mankind the common sense of the subject, in terms so plain and firm as to command their assent, and to justify ourselves in the independent stand we are compelled to take. ... Independence forever.
– *Thomas Jefferson* –

On the distinctive principles of the Government ...of the U. States, the best guides are to be found in...The Declaration of Independence, as the fundamental Act of Union of these States.
– *James Madison* –

American Revolution: "The hour is fast approaching"

Don't fire unless fired upon. But if they want a war let it begin here.
– *Captain John Parker* –

If there must be trouble let it be in my day, that my child may have peace. ... The Sun never shined on a cause of greater worth. ... Now is the seedtime of continental union, faith and honor. The least fracture now, will be like a name engraved with the point of a pin on the tender rind of a young oak; the wound would enlarge with the tree, and posterity read in it full grown characters. ... These are the times that try men's souls. The summer soldier and the sunshine patriot will, in this crisis, shrink from the service of his country; but he that stands it now, deserves the love and thanks of man and woman.

– Thomas Paine –

I only regret that I have but one life to lose for my country.
– Nathan Hale –

Our unalterable resolution would be to be free. ... Their arts may be more dangerous then their arms. Let us then renounce all treaty with them upon any score but that of total separation, and under God trust our cause to our swords. ... Contemplate the mangled bodies of your countrymen, and then say 'what should be the reward of such sacrifices?' ... If ye love wealth better than liberty, the tranquility of servitude than the animated contest of freedom, go from us in peace. We ask not your counsels or arms. Crouch down and lick the hands, which feed you. May your chains sit lightly upon you, and may posterity forget that you were our countrymen!

– Samuel Adams –

Is life so dear or peace so sweet as to be purchased at the price of chains and slavery? Forbid it, Almighty God! I know not what course others may take, but as for me, give me liberty or give me death!

– Patrick Henry –

The American war is over; but this far from being the case with the American revolution. On the contrary, nothing but the first act of the drama is closed. It remains yet to establish and perfect our new forms of government, and to prepare the principles, morals, and manners of our citizens for these forms of government after they are established and brought to perfection.

– Benjamin Rush –

Objects of the most stupendous magnitude, and measure in which the lives and liberties of millions yet unborn are intimately interested, are now before us. We are in the very midst of a revolution the most complete, unexpected and remarkable of any in the history of nations. ... But what do we mean by the American Revolution? Do we mean the American war? The Revolution was effected before the war commenced. The Revolution was in the minds and hearts of the people; a change in their religious sentiments, of their duties and obligations...This radical change in the principles, opinions, sentiments, and affections of the people was the real American Revolution.

– John Adams –

[T]he hour is fast approaching, on which the Honor and Success of this army, and the safety of our bleeding Country depend. Remember officers and Soldiers, that you are Freemen, fighting for the blessings of Liberty – that slavery will be your portion, and that of your posterity, if you do not acquit yourselves like men. ... Our cause is noble; it is the cause of mankind! ... Our own Country's Honor, all call upon us for a vigorous and manly exertion, and if we now shamefully fail, we shall become infamous to the whole world. Let us therefore rely upon the goodness of the Cause, and the aid of the supreme Being, in whose hands Victory is, to animate and encourage us to great and noble Actions - The Eyes of all our Countrymen are now upon us, and we shall have their blessings, and praises, if happily we are the instruments of saving them from the Tyranny mediated against them. Let us therefore animate and encourage each other, and show the whole world, that a Freeman contending for Liberty on his own ground is superior to any slavish mercenary on earth.

– *George Washington* –

Honor, justice, and humanity, forbid us tamely to surrender that freedom which we received from our gallant ancestors, and which our innocent posterity have a right to receive from us. We cannot endure the infamy and guilt of resigning succeeding generations to that wretchedness which inevitably awaits them if we basely entail hereditary bondage on them.

– *Thomas Jefferson* –

They accomplished a revolution which has no parallel in the annals of human society. They reared the fabrics of governments which have no model on the face of the globe. They formed the design of a great Confederacy, which it is incumbent on their successors to improve and perpetuate.

– James Madison –

Constitution of the United States: "We the people"

Our Constitution was made only for a moral and religious people. It is wholly inadequate to the government of any other. ... The only foundation of a free Constitution is pure Virtue, and if this cannot be inspired into our People. ... [T]hey may change their Rulers, and the forms of Government, but they will not obtain a lasting Liberty. ... A Constitution of Government once changed from Freedom, can never be restored. Liberty, once lost, is lost forever.

– John Adams –

The example of changing a constitution by assembling the wise men of the state, instead of assembling armies, will be worth as much to the world as the former examples we had give them. The constitution, too, which was the result of our deliberation, is unquestionably the wisest ever yet presented to men.

– Thomas Jefferson –

It is impossible for the man of pious reflection not to perceive in it [the Constitution] a finger of that Almighty hand which has been so frequently and signally extended to our relief in the critical stages of the revolution. ... Whatever may be the judgement pronounced on the competency of the architects of the Constitution, or whatever may be the destiny of the edifice prepared by them, I feel it a duty to express my profound and solemn conviction ... that there never was an assembly of men, charged with a great and arduous trust, who were more pure in their motives, or more exclusively or anxiously devoted to the object committed to them.

– James Madison –

The basis of our political systems is the right of the people to make and to alter their Constitutions of Government. But the Constitution which at any time exists, 'till changed by an explicit and authentic act of the whole People is sacredly obligatory upon all. ... Should, hereafter, those incited by the lust of power and prompted by the supineness or venality of their constituents, overleap the known barriers of this Constitution and violate the unalienable rights of humanity: it will only serve to show, that no compact among men (however provident in its construction and sacred in its ratification) can be pronounced everlasting an inviolable, and if I may so express myself, that no Wall of words, that no mound of parchment can be so formed as to stand against the sweeping torrent of boundless ambition on the side, aided by the sapping current of corrupted morals on the other.

– George Washington –

If it be asked, What is the most sacred duty and the greatest source of our security in a Republic? The answer would be, an inviolable respect for the Constitution and Laws - the first growing out of the last. ... A sacred respect for the constitutional law is the vital principle, the sustaining energy of a free government. ... The aim of every political constitution is, or ought to be, first to obtain for rulers men who possess most wisdom to discern, and most virture to pursue, the common good of the society; and in the next place, to take the most effectual precautions for keeping them virtuous whilst they continue to hold their public trust. ... The truth is, after all the declamations we have heard, that the Constitution is itself, in every rational sense, and to every useful purpose, A BILL OF RIGHTS.
      – Alexander Hamilton –

A republic, if you can keep it.
      – Benjamin Franklin –

Constitutional Interpretation: "The despotic branch"

[T]he present Constitution is the standard to which we are to cling. Under its banners, bona fide must we combat our political foes – rejecting all changes but through the channel itself provides for amendments.
      – Alexander Hamilton –

Our peculiar security is in the possession of a written Constitution. Let us not make it a blank paper by construction. ... On every question of construction carry ourselves back to the time when the Constitution was adopted, recollect the spirit manifested in the debates and instead of trying what meaning may be squeezed out of the text or invented against it, conform to the probable one in which it was passed. ... In questions of power, then, let no more be heard of confidence in man, but bind him down from mischief by the chains of the Constitution.

— *Thomas Jefferson* —

[T]here is not a syllable in the [Constitution] which directly empowers the national courts to construe the laws according to the spirit of the Constitution, or which gives them any greater latitude in this respect than may be claimed by the courts of every State. ... The Judiciary ... has no influence over either the sword or the purse; no direction either of the strength or of the wealth of the society, and can take no active resolution whatever. It may truly be said to have neither force nor will.

— *Alexander Hamilton* —

I entirely concur in the propriety of resorting to the sense in which the Constitution was accepted and ratified by the nation. In that sense alone it is the legitimate Constitution. And if that is not the guide in expounding it, there may be no security for a consistent and stable, more than for a faithful exercise of its powers.

— *James Madison* —

At the establishment of our constitutions, the judiciary bodies were supposed to be the most helpless and harmless members of the government. Experience, however, soon showed in what way they were to become the most dangerous; that the insufficiency of the means provided for their removal gave them a freehold and irresponsibility in office; that their decisions, seeming to concern individual suitors only, pass silent and unheeded by the public at large; that these decisions, nevertheless, become law by precedent, sapping, by little and little, the foundations of the constitution, and working its change by construction, before any one has perceived that that invisible and helpless worm has been busily employed in consuming its substance.
... [T]he opinion which gives to the judges the right to decide what laws are constitutional and what not, not only for themselves, in their, own sphere of action, but for the Legislature and Executive also in their spheres, would make the Judiciary a despotic branch. ... The judiciary...is the subtle corps of sappers and miners constantly working under ground to undermine the foundations of our confederated fabric. They are construing our constitution from a co-ordination of a general and special government to a general and supreme one alone ... until all shall be usurped from the States, and the government of all be consolidated into one. ... One single object ... [will merit] the endless gratitude of the society: that of restraining the judges from usurping legislation.

– *Thomas Jefferson* –

The first and governing maxim in the interpretation of a statute is to discover the meaning of those who made it.
– *James Wilson* –

The constitution of the United States is to receive a reasonable interpretation of its language, and its powers, keeping in view the objects and purposes, for which those powers were conferred. By a reasonable interpretation, we mean, that in case the words are susceptible of two different senses, the one strict, the other more enlarged, that should be adopted, which is most consonant with the apparent objects and intent of the Constitution.
– *Joseph Story* –

Federalism: "Powers not delegated to the United States"

I consider the foundation of the Constitution as laid on this ground that 'all powers not delegated to the United States, by the Constitution, nor prohibited by it to the states, are reserved to the states or to the people.' To take a single step beyond the boundaries thus specially drawn around the powers of Congress, is to take possession of a boundless field of power, not longer susceptible of any definition. ... [T]he States can best govern our home concerns and the general government our foreign ones. I wish, therefore ... never to see all offices transferred to Washington, where, further withdrawn from the eyes of the people, they may more secretly be bought and sold at market.
– *Thomas Jefferson* –

The powers delegated by the proposed Constitution to the federal government are few and defined. Those which are to remain in the State governments are numerous and indefinite. ... The operations of the federal government will be most extensive and important in times of war and danger; those of the State governments, in times of peace and security.
– James Madison –

This balance between the National and State governments ought to be dwelt on with peculiar attention, as it is of the utmost importance. It forms a double security to the people. If one encroaches on their rights they will find a powerful protection in the other. Indeed, they will both be prevented from overpassing their constitutional limits by a certain rivalship, which will ever subsist between them.
– Alexander Hamilton –

[T]he powers of the general government will be, and indeed must be, principally employed upon external objects, such as war, peace, negotiations with foreign powers, and foreign commerce. In its internal operations it can touch but few objects, except to introduce regulations beneficial to the commerce, intercourse, and other relations, between the states, and to lay taxes for the common good. The powers of the states, on the other hand, extend to all objects, which, in the ordinary course of affairs, concern the lives, and liberties, and property of the people, and the internal order, improvement, and prosperity of the state.
– Joseph Story –

Our Creator: "The Law of Nature and Nature's God"

The belief in a God All Powerful wise and good, is so essential to the moral order of the world and to the happiness of man, that arguments which enforce it cannot be drawn from too many sources nor adapted with too much solicitude to the different characters and capacities impressed with it.
– James Madison –

And can the liberties of a nation be thought secure when we have removed their only firm basis, a conviction in the minds of the people that these liberties are the gift of God? That they are not to be violated but with his wrath? Indeed I tremble for my country when I reflect that God is just: that his justice cannot sleep for ever. ... The doctrines of Jesus are simple, and tend all to the happiness of mankind.
Thomas Jefferson –

The Bible is the best of all books, for it is the word of God and teaches us the way to be happy in this world and in the next. Continue therefore to read it and to regulate your life by its precepts.
– John Jay

Religion is the only solid Base of morals and that Morals are the only possible Support of free governments. ... [T]herefore education should teach the precepts of religion and the duties of man towards God.
– Gouverneur Morris –

It is the duty of all men in society, publicly, and at stated seasons, to worship the SUPREME BEING, the great Creator and Preserver of the universe. And no subject shall be hurt, molested, or restrained, in his person, liberty, or estate, for worshipping GOD in the manner most agreeable to the dictates of his own conscience; or for his religious profession or sentiments; provided he doth not disturb the public peace, or obstruct others in their religious worship. ... Statesmen ... may plan and speculate for Liberty, but it is Religion and Morality alone, which can establish the Principles upon which Freedom can securely stand.

– *John Adams* –

[O]nly a virtuous people are capable of freedom. As nations become corrupt and vicious, they have more need of masters. ... I have lived, Sir, a long time; and the longer I live, the more convincing proofs I see of this Truth, that God governs in the Affairs of Men. And if a Sparrow cannot fall to the Ground without his Notice, is it probable that an Empire can rise without his Aid? ... We have been assured...in the Sacred Writings, that "except the Lord build the House, they labor in vain that build it." I firmly believe this...

– *Benjamin Franklin* –

[A]ll men are equally bound by the laws of nature, or to speak more properly, the laws of the Creator. ... Religion and good morals are the only solid foundation of public liberty and happiness.

– *Samuel Adams* –

It is the duty of all Nations to acknowledge the providence of Almighty God, to obey his will, to be grateful for his benefits, and humbly to implore his protection and favors. ... The propitious smiles of Heaven can never be expected on a nation that disregards the eternal rules of order and right, which Heaven itself has ordained. ... The Hand of providence has been so conspicuous in all this, that he must be worse than an infidel that lacks faith, and more than wicked, that has not gratitude enough to acknowledge his obligations. ... The foundations of our national policy will be laid in the pure and immutable principles of private morality. ... [W]here is the security for property, for reputation, for life, if the sense of religious obligation deserts the oaths...?

– *George Washington* –

[T]he only foundation for a useful education in a republic is to be laid in religion. Without this there can be no virtue, and without virtue there can be no liberty, and liberty is the object and life of all republican governments.

– *Benjamin Rush* –

The law of nature and the law of revelation are both Divine: they flow, though in different channels, from the same adorable source. It is indeed preposterous to separate them from each other. ... Far from being rivals or enemies, religion and law are twin sisters, friends, and mutual assistants. Indeed, these two sciences run into each other. The divine law, as discovered by reason and the moral sense, forms an essential part of both.

– *James Wilson* –

Liberty: "Proclaim liberty throughout the land"

They that can give up essential liberty to purchase a little temporary safety, deserve neither liberty nor safety.
– Benjamin Franklin –

A nation which can prefer disgrace to danger is prepared for a master, and deserves one! ... Of those men who have overturned the liberties of republics, the greatest number have begun their career by paying an obsequious court to the people, commencing demagogues and ending tyrants.
– Alexander Hamilton –

Liberty must at all hazards be supported. We have a right to it, derived from our Maker. ... Our obligations to our country never cease but with our lives. ... [W]e should be unfaithful to ourselves if we should ever lose sight of the danger to our liberties if anything partial or extraneous should infect the purity of our free, fair, virtuous, and independent elections.
– John Adams –

The God who gave us life, gave us liberty at the same time; the hand of force may destroy, but cannot disjoin them. ... Love your neighbor as yourself and your country more than yourself. ... The boisterous sea of liberty is never without a wave. ... I have sworn upon the altar of God, eternal hostility against every form of tyranny over the mind of man. ... The tree of liberty must be refreshed from time to time with the blood of patriots and tyrants. It is its natural manure.
– Thomas Jefferson –

Without liberty, law loses its nature and its name, and becomes oppression. Without law, liberty also loses its nature and its name, and becomes licentiousness.

– James Wilson –

Is the relinquishment of the trial by jury and the liberty of the press necessary for your liberty? Will the abandonment of your most sacred rights tend to the security of your liberty? Liberty, the greatest of all earthly blessings – give us that precious jewel, and you may take every things else! … Guard with jealous attention the public liberty. Suspect every one who approaches that jewel.

– Patrick Henry –

The value of liberty was thus enhanced in our estimation by the difficulty of its attainment, and the worth of characters appreciated by the trial of adversity. ... The name of American, which belongs to you, in your national capacity, must always exalt the just pride of Patriotism, more than any appellation derived from local discriminations. ... Guard against the impostures of pretended patriotism. ... It should be the highest ambition of every American to extend his views beyond himself, and to bear in mind that his conduct will not only affect himself, his country, and his immediate posterity; but that its influence may be co-extensive with the world, and stamp political happiness or misery on ages yet unborn.

– George Washington –

He that would make his own liberty secure, must guard
even his enemy from oppression; for if he violates this duty,
he establishes a precedent that will reach to himself.
– Thomas Paine –

Economy and Taxes:
"Ignorance of the nature of coin"

The natural effort of every individual to better his own
condition is so powerful that it is alone, and without any
assistance, not only capable of carrying on the society
to wealth and prosperity, but of surmounting a hundred
impertinent obstructions with which the folly of human
laws too often encumbers its operations. ... Nobody but a
beggar chooses to depend chiefly upon the benevolence of
his fellow-citizens.
– Adam Smith –

All the perplexities, confusion and distress in America arise
not from defects in their Constitution or Confederation, nor
from want of honor or virtue, so much as downright ignorance of the nature of coin, credit, and circulation.
– John Adams –

If duties are too high, they lessen the consumption; the
collection is eluded; and the product to the treasury is
not so great as when they are confined within proper and
moderate bounds.
– Alexander Hamilton –

I am for a government rigorously frugal and simple. Were we directed from Washington when to sow, when to reap, we should soon want bread. ... A rigid economy of the public contributions and absolute interdiction of all use-less expenses will go far towards keeping the government honest and unoppressive. ... A wise and frugal government ... shall not take from the mouth of labor the bread it has earned. ... I think we have more machinery of government than is necessary, too many parasites living on the labor of the industrious. ... Would it not be better to simplify the system of taxation rather than to spread it over such a vari-ety of subjects and pass through so many new hands. ... To take from one, because it is thought his own industry and that of his fathers has acquired too much, in order to spare to others, who, or whose fathers, have not exercised equal industry and skill, is to violate arbitrarily the first principle of association, the guarantee to everyone the free exercise of his industry and the fruits acquired by it.

– Thomas Jefferson

We are in danger of being overwhelmed with irredeemable paper, mere paper, representing not gold nor silver; no sir, representing nothing but broken promises, bad faith, bank-rupt corporations, cheated creditors and a ruined people. ... Of all contrivances for cheating the laboring classes of man-kind, none has been more effective than that which deludes them with paper money.

– Daniel Webster –

I cannot undertake to lay my finger on that article of the Constitution which granted a right to Congress of expending, on objects of benevolence, the money of their constituents. ... A just security to property is not afforded by that government, under which unequal taxes oppress one species of property and reward another species. ... The apportionment of taxes on the various descriptions of property is an act which seems to require the most exact impartiality; yet there is, perhaps, no legislative act in which greater opportunity and temptation are given to a predominant party to trample on the rules of justice.

– *James Madison* –

An unlimited power to tax involves, necessarily, a power to destroy; because there is a limit beyond which no institution and no property can bear taxation.

– *John Marshall* –

Our new Constitution is now established, and has an appearance that promises permanency; but in this world nothing can be said to be certain, except death and taxes. ... I am for doing good to the poor, but I differ in opinion of the means. I think the best way of doing good to the poor, is not making them easy in poverty, but leading or driving them out of it. In my youth I travelled much, and I observed in different countries, that the more public provisions were made for the poor, the less they provided for themselves, and of course became poorer. And, on the contrary, the less was done for them, the more they did for themselves, and became richer.

– *Benjamin Franklin* –

In a general sense, all contributions imposed by the government upon individuals for the service of the state, are called taxes, by whatever name they may be known, whether by the name of tribute, tythe, tallage, impost, duty, gabel, custom, subsidy, aid, supply, excise, or other name.
– Joseph Story –

Posterity: "Enlighten the people"

Let the American youth never forget, that they possess a noble inheritance, bought by the toils, and sufferings, and blood of their ancestors; and capacity, if wisely improved, and faithfully guarded, of transmitting to their latest posterity all the substantial blessings of life, the peaceful enjoyment of liberty, property, religion, and independence.
– Joseph Story –

It is an object of vast magnitude that systems of education should be adopted and pursued which may not only diffuse a knowledge of the sciences but may implant in the minds of the American youth the principles of virtue and of liberty and inspire them with just and liberal ideas of government and with an inviolable attachment to their own country.
– Noah Webster –

Law and liberty cannot rationally become the objects of our love, unless they first become the objects of our knowledge.
– James Wilson –

Liberty cannot be preserved without a general knowledge among the people, who have a right, from the frame of their nature, to knowledge, as their great Creator, who does nothing in vain, has given them understandings, and a desire to know. ... Children should be educated and instructed in the principles of freedom.

– John Adams –

No people will tamely surrender their Liberties, nor can any be easily subdued, when knowledge is diffused and Virtue is preserved. On the Contrary, when People are universally ignorant, and debauched in their Manners, they will sink under their own weight without the Aid of foreign Invaders.

– Samuel Adams –

Enlighten the people, generally, and tyranny and oppressions of body and mind will vanish like spirits at the dawn of day. ... If a nation expects to be ignorant – and free – in a state of civilization, it expects what never was and never will be.

– Thomas Jefferson –

A popular Government, without popular information, or the means of acquiring it, is but a Prologue to a Farce or a Tragedy; or, perhaps both. Knowledge will forever govern ignorance: And a people who mean to be their own Governors, must arm themselves with the power which knowledge gives. ... What spectacle can be more edifying or more seasonable, than that of Liberty and Learning, each leaning on the other for their mutual & surest support?

– James Madison –

Essential Liberty Resources

These, and many other resources are available online at
www.essentiallibertyproject.us/resources

The Code of Hammurabi (ca. 1727-1680 BC)
The Ten Commandments (ca. 1447 BC)
The Constitutions of Clarendon (1164)
The Magna Carta (June 15, 1215)
The Declaration of Arbroath (1320)
Privileges Granted Christopher Columbus (1492)
Charter to Sir Walter Raleigh (March 25, 1584)
Colonial Charters (1606-1732)
Mayflower Compact (November 11, 1620)
Surrender of the Great Charter of New England (1635)
Confederation of the United Colonies (May 19, 1643)
The First Thanksgiving Proclamation (1676)
English Bill of Rights (1689)
John Locke: The Second Treatise of Government (1689)
Resolutions of the Stamp Act (1765)
Anonymous Account of the Boston Massacre (March 5, 1770)
Declaration of the First Continental Congress (October 14, 1774)
Give Me Liberty or Give Me Death! (March 23, 1775)
Samuel Adams on American Independence (August 1, 1776)
Common Sense – Thomas Paine (1776)
The Rights of Man – Thomas Paine (1792)
State Constitutions (1776-1778)
The Federalist Papers (1787)
The Anti-Federalist Papers (1787)

ABOUT THE PATRIOT POST

The Patriot Post is a highly acclaimed journal providing incontrovertible constitutional rebuttal to contemporary political, social and media protagonists on the Left. Join the ranks of hundreds of thousands of American Patriots who read this brief, informative and entertaining analysis of the week's most significant news, policy and opinion.

It's Right. It's Free. Subscribe at PatriotPost.US

"The best Websites wield remarkable influence in the marketplace of ideas. *The Patriot Post* is a 'must read' for informed conservatives." – Dr. Ed Feulner Jr., President, Heritage Foundation

"The vision and legacy of the Reagan Revolution flourish on the pages of *The Patriot*." – Michael Reagan, Author and Syndicated Radio Host

"Daniel Webster was right, 'God grants liberty only to those who love it and are always ready to guard and defend it.' *Patriot Post* readers understand that commission." – Dr. Larry Arnn, Author and Constitutional Scholar

"Simply put, *The Patriot Post* cuts through the clutter and delivers timely, accurate, and colorful accounts of the week's most important news and policy issues. It's a mandatory read." – Dr. Richard (Dick) Armey, Former House Majority Leader

"*The Patriot's* message provides a critical touchstone for those inside the Beltway who have forgotten whom they serve." – Former Senator Fred Thompson

"*The Patriot Post* is leading a well-organized charge into the world of Internet politics." – Harvard Political Review

"*The Patriot* is leading the charge in the battle to restore America's values – a vital ally on the front...." – Dr. Bill Bennett, Author

"*The Patriot* is an indispensable resource for sound conservative opinion." – R. Emmett Tyrrell Jr., Editor in Chief, American Spectator

"*The Patriot Post* recalls the noble tradition of our Founders. 'Publius' would have admired and endorsed *The Patriot*, as do I." Dr. Alan Keyes, Author and Constitutional Scholar

"*The Patriot* interprets current issues in the conservative context of history." – Cal Thomas, Author

"Thank you for your confidence in, and efforts to sustain the Reagan legacy." – Howard Baker, Former White House Chief of Staff

"Liberals say and do so many nutty things. *The Patriot* puts them all in a nutshell – easy to crack and fun to read." – Marvin Olasky, Senior Fellow, Acton Institute

Support
The Essential Liberty Project

The mission of the Essential Liberty Project is to support the restoration of constitutional integrity and Rule of Law. Part of that mission is a critical and timely educational initiative to distribute millions of Essential Liberty pocket reference guides.

As a primer on liberty, "endowed by our Creator" and codified by our Founders in the Declaration of Independence and the U.S. Constitution, these guides have a proven record as an essential resource for Patriots of all ages.

We invite you to join the ranks of Patriots advancing our legacy of liberty by purchasing and/or sponsoring these exceptional guides for distribution to students, grassroots organizations, civic clubs, political alliances, military and public service personnel, and other groups across the nation. Support Essential Liberty today!

For more information, or to
Support the Essential Liberty Project online:
EssentialLibertyProject.US

Support the Essential Liberty Project by mail:
Essential Liberty Project
PO Box 407
Chattanooga, Tennessee 37401 USA
(Make checks payable to "Essential Liberty Project")